The Battle of MANILA BAY

The Battle of MANILA BAY

The Spanish-American War in the Philippines

By Robert Conroy

The Macmillan Company, New York
Collier-Macmillan Limited, London

Copyright © Robert Conroy 1968
Copyright © The Macmillan Company 1968

All rights reserved. No part of this book may be reproduced or transmitted in any form or by any means, electronic or mechanical, including photocopying, recording or by any information storage and retrieval system, without permission in writing from the Publisher.

The Macmillan Company, New York
Collier-Macmillan Canada, Ltd., Toronto, Ontario
Library of Congress catalog card number: 68-12068
Printed in the United States of America
FIRST PRINTING

Maps by Rafael Palacios

PICTURE CREDITS: Culver Pictures, 9, 10 (top), 10 (bottom), 44; Dewey, Adelbert M., *The Life and Letters of Admiral Dewey*, 28, 48, 65, 85; *Harper's Weekly*, July 30, 1898, 65; Historical Pictures Service–Chicago, title page, viii, 2, 19, 20, 36–37, 41, 42–43, 60, 63, 68, 74, 80, 82; King, W. N., *The Story of the War of 1898*, 30, 31; Library of Congress, 12–13; The Mariner's Museum, Newport News, Va., 23, 24; National Archives, 70–71, 72–73, 75; Radio Times Hulton Picture Library, 15; The Smithsonian Institution, 50–51; U.S. Naval Academy Museum, 34, 40; U.S. Navy, 47, 56, 57. Picture research by Patricia Crum.

Cover illustration, Culver Pictures.

For Syma Ebbin

Oh, dewey was the morning
Upon the first of May,
And Dewey was the Admiral
Down in Manila Bay.
And dewey were the Regent's eyes
Them orbs of royal blue,
And dew we feel discouraged?
I dew not think we dew!

—*The Minneapolis Tribune*
October, 1898

CONTENTS

1. "A Brave Set of Fellows . . ." 1

2. "Your Excellency Knows That I Have No Torpedoes" 17

3. "You May Fire When You Are Ready, Gridley" 32

4. To the Victor . . . 59

Chronology 77

5. The Sands of Time 79

For Further Reading 86

Index 87

1. "A BRAVE SET OF FELLOWS..."

Saturday, April 30, 1898. Beneath a cloudless sky, the waters of Subic Bay on the west coast of Luzon, main island in the Philippine archipelago, are still. Late afternoon sunlight sparkles brilliantly against the greenish surface of the bay and the deeper blue of the South China Sea beyond. From the dark green jungles near-by come the cries of monkeys and brightly colored birds, alarmed, perhaps, by a strange sight. For the accustomed tropical sleepiness of this scene is disturbed today by the presence of nine gray-painted and grim-looking ships. These are the cruisers *Olympia*, *Baltimore*, *Boston*, and *Raleigh*, the gunboats *Petrel*, and *Concord*, the revenue cutter *Hugh McCulloch*, and the transports *Nanshan* and *Zafiro*. The Asiatic squadron of the United States Navy, under the command of Commodore George Dewey, is in Subic Bay stripped for action, crews at battle stations, looking for Spain's

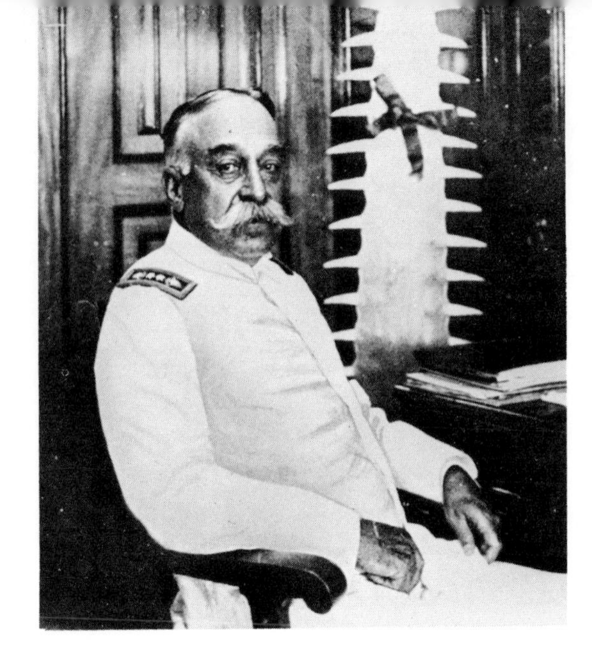

George Dewey, commander of the Asiatic squadron of the United States Navy

Far Eastern fleet. So far it has encountered only a small Spanish fishing schooner whose frightened captain tells the Americans that he has no idea where the Spanish fleet is. But if the Spanish warships are not in Subic Bay then they must be waiting in Manila Bay behind the mine- and torpedo-infested waters around the island of Corregidor. Commodore Dewey calls a council of war aboard his flagship, the USS *Olympia*.

Joseph L. Stickney, war correspondent for the *New York Herald* (and temporary aide to the commodore) later recalled: "Commodore Dewey stopped his flagship and made signal for commanding officers to repair on board. When every gig had been called away, and the captain of each ship was steering in solitary state toward the *Olympia* no one needed to be told that we were on the eve of battle."

"They're comin'," muttered an old seaman standing next to Stickney, "to hear the old man's last words before we go at the dons."

"Not his *last* words," one of the younger men chaffed.

"Perhaps not his," the grizzled veteran insisted, "but it's near our last words some of us are. There'll be many an eye will look at the sunset tonight that'll never see another!"

Nor were the old seaman's apprehensions ill founded. As the captains who gathered at the conference table in the *Olympia*'s main cabin understood, since the Spanish fleet had elected to fight in Manila Bay, the United States squadron was faced with but two alternatives—neither of them very attractive. In order to get at the Spanish warships they would have to pass the heavily fortified island of Corregidor at the mouth of Manila Bay. They could either bombard and silence Corregidor's heavy batteries, or they could try to slip past the island at night—and run the risk of destruction on the mines and torpedoes with which the channels into Manila Bay were reportedly infested. But Commodore Dewey's mind was already made up.

"Gentlemen," he told the assembled captains, "I was brought up under that grand old man, Admiral Farragut, and when he had a task like this, he went straight through and did it. We will go into Manila Bay tonight and if there are any mines in our path the flagship will clear them away for you." The "council" had ended.

As Captain Nehemiah Dyer clambered back aboard his cruiser, the *Baltimore*, he turned to his watch officer, Lieutenant John Ellicott, and said: "Stand by to get under way. We are going to try something tonight never attempted since the Civil War." Captain Dyer, thinking of Farragut's dash past the shore batteries and through the mine fields into Mobile Bay thirty-three years before, explained that the squadron, proceeding in single file with the flagship *Olympia* leading the way, each ship guided through the night only by a small, boxed-in lantern on the stern of the ship in front, would attempt to sneak past the heavy shore batteries of

Corregidor and through the mine fields into Manila Bay.

At about 7 P.M. the squadron was once again under way.

As night closed in with tropical swiftness a bright quarter moon rose. From his position at the taffrail on the *Olympia*'s stern, correspondent Stickney "could just get a faint suggestion of a ghostly shape where the *Baltimore* grimly held her course on our port quarter . . ."

Aboard the *Baltimore*, Lieutenant Ellicott was going through his papers, burning some and sorting others. The *Baltimore*'s young chaplain came into Ellicott's cabin and remarked: "How can you be so composed? You don't seem to realize the horrors ahead of us; the crashing shells; the mangled bodies; the ship perhaps on fire and sinking; the . . . " But the chaplain's worries were silenced by the sudden appearance of assistant engineer E. L. Beach who entered Ellicott's cabin, slapped the chaplain on the back, and said: "Brace up, chaplain. Remember that you represent God in this ship. If you fear all that, go to your room and pray for us."

It was nearly midnight when the hills of Manila loomed dimly ahead through the moonlight. Ahead too loomed the dark mass of dreaded Corregidor and its sister island, El Fraile. The squadron's crews had been at their guns since 10 P.M., called there not by bugles, but by stealthy whispers. Tension was nearing the breaking point. Would the guns of Corregidor and the batteries of El Fraile erupt suddenly and rain a cross fire of heavy shells onto the American ships? Would a blinding flash split the night to mark where the *Olympia* had exploded against a mine?

Suddenly, a shower of sparks flew from the smokestack of the revenue cutter *McCulloch*. Surely the Spaniards must

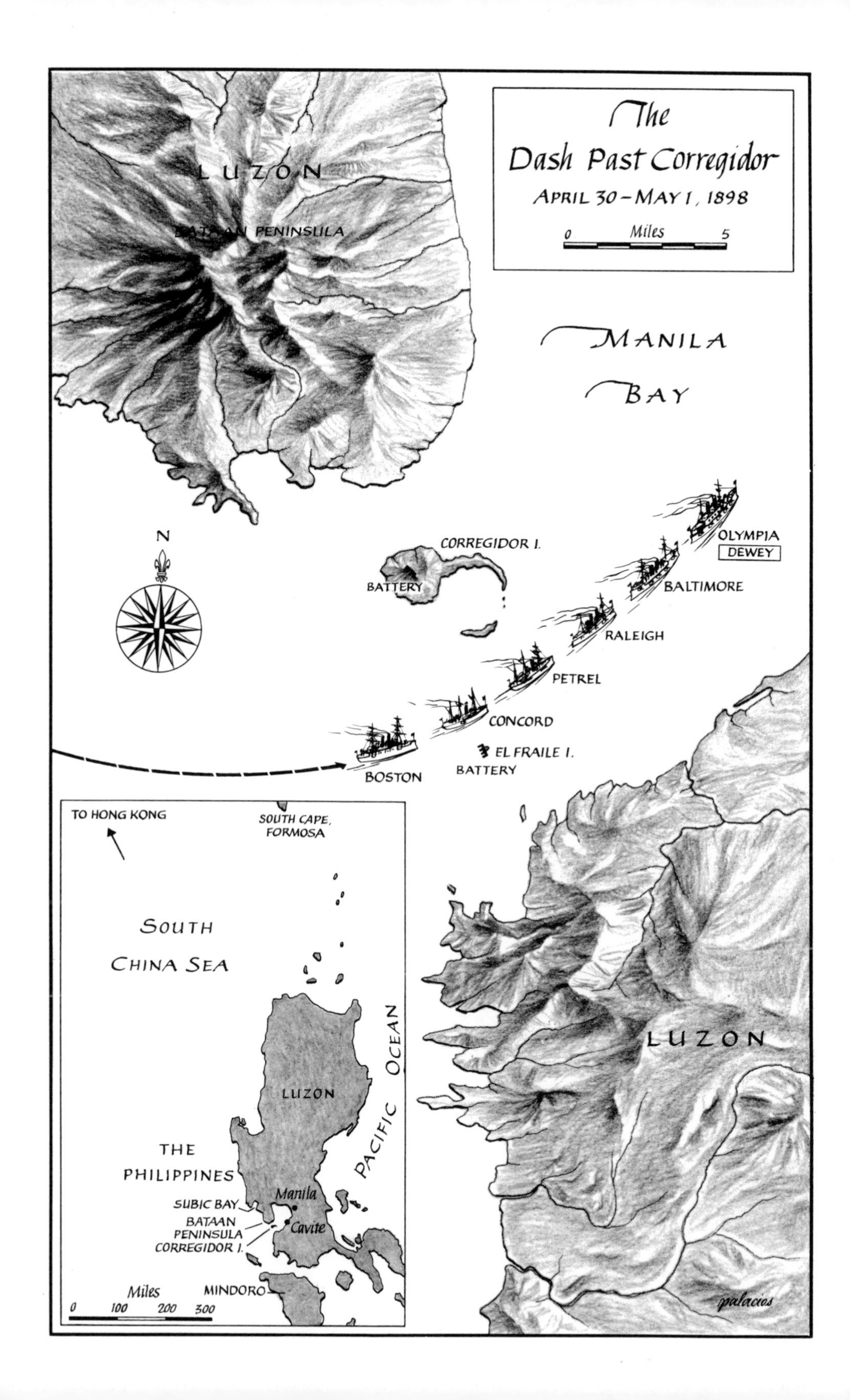
The Dash Past Corregidor
APRIL 30 – MAY 1, 1898
0 Miles 5
LUZON
BATAAN PENINSULA
MANILA BAY
N
CORREGIDOR I.
BATTERY
OLYMPIA
DEWEY
BALTIMORE
RALEIGH
PETREL
CONCORD
EL FRAILE I.
BATTERY
BOSTON
LUZON
TO HONG KONG
SOUTH CAPE, FORMOSA
SOUTH CHINA SEA
PACIFIC OCEAN
LUZON
THE PHILIPPINES
SUBIC BAY
Manila
BATAAN PENINSULA
Cavite
CORREGIDOR I.
Miles
MINDORO
0 100 200 300
palacios

have seen that! The men on the bridge of the *Olympia* waited tensely for a shell from the silent darkness ahead. Sensing the increasing tension, Commodore Dewey turned to the *Olympia*'s captain, Charles Gridley, and remarked in a loud voice: "A fine night for a smoke, eh, Gridley? It's a pity we can't light up." That lessened the anxiety and the men on the *Olympia*'s bridge breathed a little more easily.

Not everyone in the American squadron was tense. Resting on his berth in his cabin aboard the small gunboat *Petrel*, Lieutenant Bradley Fiske could not stifle a yawn. His roommate, Lieutenant E. M. Hughes, reproached him: "Bradley, that is very impolite, and besides, it is a bad sign, because yawns in the evening mean tremors in the morning." Fiske did not reply. He was thinking about how flat he would be if the *Petrel* struck a mine and he was squashed up against the steel deck just two feet above his face.

Aboard the *Baltimore*, Lieutenant Ellicott saw a huge rock loom suddenly to starboard. "El Fraile!" the navigator exclaimed, "the *Olympia* must have almost run into it."

"Oh no," Captain Dyer remarked. "The commodore intended it so. He's an old hand at crossing mine fields and figured that if there was a gate through this one it would be close to that rock."

Only a tense silence greeted Captain Dyer's explanation. Then suddenly the *Baltimore*'s signal officer exclaimed: "There's a ship on fire astern of us!"

It was the *McCulloch*'s smokestack, once again showering sparks from the soft coal she was burning. Aboard the *Olympia* someone on the bridge growled: "Well if someone don't see that, the whole island must be asleep!"

But someone had seen it. Slowly a rocket arced through

the night and exploded over Corregidor. It was followed by the whistle of two heavy shells as the Spanish batteries on El Fraile opened fire on the American ships. "Well, well," Commodore Dewey exclaimed, "they did wake up at last!"

Guns on the *Boston*, the *Concord*, the *Raleigh*, and the *McCulloch* returned the Spanish fire, silencing the battery on El Fraile with a few shots. Then once again darkness and silence enveloped the squadron.

The Americans were past Corregidor and El Fraile now, past the heavy shore batteries and the dreaded mine fields. Twenty-four miles away the city of Manila and the Spanish fleet awaited the arrival of the audacious squadron. It was shortly after midnight on May 1, 1898. Commodore Dewey signaled his squadron to reduce speed to four knots. He wanted to arrive at Manila in daylight. He had just accomplished a deed as daring as any his old commander, Admiral Farragut, had ever attempted, and, his confidence in the nerve of his men justified, the commodore stepped into his cabin for a few hours of sleep.

Commodore Dewey and the "Splendid Little War"

The commodore who could so coolly retire for a nap as his ships steamed toward combat was a remarkable man and he was engaged on a remarkable mission. Born on December 27, 1837, at Montpelier, Vermont, George Dewey was a spirited boy—in fact today his conduct might be considered to verge on delinquency. But in the Vermont of the 1850's such behavior was dealt with summarily and directly. In later years Dewey was to remember gratefully the thrashings he received from his teacher. Dewey wanted, originally, to go to West Point, but he failed of appointment. Instead he went to the U.S. Naval Academy at Annapolis, from which he graduated in 1861. During the Civil War he served with distinction under Farragut on the Mississippi and Admiral David Porter at Fort Fisher, emerging from the holocaust with the rank of lieutenant commander. He had a reputation for coolness under fire and for enforcing stern discipline.

The years of peace after the Civil War, during which the U.S. Navy was allowed to decline to a level on which it could not hope to meet the navy of Chile on equal terms, brought painfully slow promotion to Dewey. They brought also, his first marriage, which ended tragically with the death of his wife in childbirth in 1872. He served on the Lighthouse Inspection and Maintenance Commission and on various European cruises, reaching the rank of captain in 1884.

In 1896, at the age of fifty-eight, only four years from retirement, Dewey was finally given the rank of commodore, after three years' service as president of the Bureau of Inspection and Survey. Although this work enabled him to become familiar with the new steel cruisers and battleships which were beginning to emerge from the nation's shipyards during the 80's and 90's, it seemed that younger men would be commanding them. The commodore remarked to a friend in 1896: "There will be no war before I retire from the navy, and I'll simply join the great majority of naval men, and be known in history only by consulting the records of the Navy Department, as 'George Dewey, who entered the navy in 1854 and retired as rear admiral at the age limit.' " Two years later the United States was at war with Spain.

During the summer of 1898, John Hay, the United States

Ambassador to England, wrote to Theodore Roosevelt: "It has been a splendid little war; begun with the highest motives . . ." To later Americans the war was to seem somewhat less than splendid, and its motives quite mistaken, if not absolutely base.

Commodore Dewey on shipboard

LEFT: *President William McKinley.*
BELOW: *Theodore Roosevelt, Assistant Secretary of the Navy*

There were many factors which brought about the Spanish-American War. On a popular level the war was a crusade to liberate the long-suffering island of Cuba from Spanish misrule and tyranny. The war fever was whipped up and nourished by the emergence of "yellow journalism," too —in fact, in later years, publisher William Randolph Hearst was to claim that the conflict was "his" war. But in this Hearst was overstating his influence. Nor was the war brought about by business interests—they opposed it, by and large. But the conservative Republican and Democratic politicians who represented the business community perceived that war might provide a means of diverting the rising storm of popular protest against harsh business exploitation of American labor and resources. And, perhaps of decisive importance, there was a growing desire among all segments of American society to see the United States act like a great world power, complete with a powerful navy, overseas bases, and a belligerent foreign policy. Spain, the weakest opponent American jingoism could find on the international horizon, seemed a likely first victim.

Assistant Secretary of the Navy Theodore Roosevelt, with the support of young Senator Henry Cabot Lodge, had long before determined that if war with Spain broke out (he devoutly hoped it would), then the United States would seize the Philippine Islands, Spain's great Asiatic colony. Before 1898, most Americans, including President William McKinley (as he later confessed) would have been hard put to find the Philippines on a map of the world. But Roosevelt and Lodge looked upon the archipelago as a promising base for American trade and sea power in the Pacific. Since the summer of 1897, Roosevelt had been gathering data about the

The destruction of the USS Maine *in Havana harbor*

Spanish defenses of the Philippines. The small American Asiatic squadron was reinforced and, in the fall of 1897, Commodore George Dewey was sent to command it. Immediately, the commodore began an intensive study of Philip-

pine harbors and the quality of the Spanish Far Eastern fleet.

On February 15, 1898, the United States battleship *Maine* blew up and sank with 260 of her crew while anchored in Havana harbor. Although it was overwhelmingly improbable that the *Maine* had been sunk by the Spanish authorities in

Cuba (Spain was desperately trying to avoid war with the United States), an enraged American public opinion did not hesitate to blame the Spaniards. "Remember the *Maine*, to hell with Spain!" became the war cry which obliterated reason.

A fleet was sent to blockade Cuba and Roosevelt dispatched a cable to Dewey on February 25, 1898, which read:

"Order the squadron, except the *Monocacy*, to Hong Kong. Keep full of coal. In the event declaration of war Spain, your duty will be to see that the Spanish squadron does not leave the Asiatic coast, and then offensive operations in Philippine Islands. Keep *Olympia* until further orders. Roosevelt."

Commodore Dewey immediately set about preparing his small squadron for war. The supply ships *Nanshan* and *Zafiro* were purchased from the British and loaded with coal. Officers studied charts of the Philippine Islands while crew men hastily painted their gleaming white vessels grim gray. Tension mounted as the now inevitable declaration of war was awaited. On April 22nd, the cruiser *Baltimore* arrived at Hong Kong loaded with ammunition. Within forty-eight hours she had been dry-docked, had her bottom scraped and painted, and was made ready for war—none too soon, since the next day, April 23rd, Dewey was notified by the British governor of Hong Kong that the United States had declared war on Spain. Since Britain was neutral, Dewey's squadron would have to leave Hong Kong within two days.

To British naval officers at Hong Kong, Dewey's position seemed all but hopeless. He was preparing to meet a fleet which, on paper, looked as powerful as his own; and in

A view of Hong Kong in the late 1800's

order to even come to grips with that fleet he would have to brave the mines, torpedoes, and heavy shore batteries of one of the world's most heavily defended ports—Manila. If Dewey lost the battle, or even if he failed to win a completely decisive victory, he would be utterly helpless, without supplies or ammunition, thousands of miles from any American base. But the British liked the quiet commodore and his plucky little squadron. As the American ships sailed from Hong Kong on April 25th, British sailors manned the rigging of their own ships and gave cheer after ringing cheer to the departing squadron. But in the officers' clubs ashore, Her Majesty's sea dogs shook their heads regretfully and said: "A brave set of fellows, but unhappily we shall never see them again."

When, a few days later, on May 1st, a British steamer passed through a mass of floating shutters and hatches and tables and chairs in the South China Sea, it seemed that Dewey must have fought and lost a great battle. The British captain had no way of knowing that this wreckage had been purposely thrown overboard by the American squadron as it stripped for action—or that at that very moment, the terrors of Corregidor and El Fraile behind them, the American ships were silently emerging from the morning mist into Manila Bay.

2. "YOUR EXCELLENCY KNOWS THAT I HAVE NO TORPEDOES"

Rear Admiral Patricio Montojo y Pasarón, commander of the Spanish Far Eastern fleet, knew that the American squadron was entering Manila Bay that morning. He had known when they entered and left Subic Bay the day before, had known when they passed Corregidor and El Fraile during the night. In fact, he had been expecting the Americans to come for more than two years. And those two years had seen a fevered fight between Admiral Montojo and the Spanish authorities in Madrid for supplies, ships, ammunition, plans, orders—a fight Montojo had steadily lost. But the most important battle, from the admiral's viewpoint, had been lost anyway, during November of 1896. For it was then that Admiral Montojo had been called from his position as director of matériel at the Spanish Ministry of Marine and ordered to take command of the fleet in the Philippines.

Montojo had protested to his chief, Admiral Beranger; had fulminated, begged, done everything in his power to avoid the appointment. War with the United States was very clearly on the horizon in 1896, and Montojo knew he was being selected as a sacrificial victim to honor. In the end he had no choice. He arrived at his new post on January 7, 1897, to take command of the collection of naval antiques which Spain called her Far Eastern fleet.

Admiral Montojo was born at El Ferrol, Spain, on September 7, 1839, into a family which sent no less than thirty-two of its members to the Spanish Navy from 1800 to 1860. He entered the Royal Naval College at Cádiz in 1852, and by 1860 had trained and served in Cuba, Mexico, the Atlantic, and the Mediterranean Sea. Although he was two years younger than George Dewey, Montojo was already in the Philippines on his first voyage to the Far East in 1860, when Midshipman Dewey was still attending classes at the Naval Academy. Montojo took part in one of the endless Spanish campaigns against the Filipino insurrectionists in 1860, returned to Spain in 1864, filled out his time between sea commands and desk duty at the Ministry of Marine, reached the grade of rear admiral in 1891, commanded Spanish naval forces at Puerto Rico from 1892 to 1894—and received what he considered to be the death sentence of the Philippine command in 1896. But he knew his duty—and he tried mightily to perform it, in the face of a home government which seemed bent on its own destruction.

Spain, in 1898, was nominally a constitutional monarchy. There was a parliament, the *Cortés,* there were elections, cabinets, and prime ministers. And there was the twelve-year-old king, Alfonso XIII, too young to rule, his power exercised by his strong-willed mother, Maria Cristina, acting

Alfonso XIII, King of Spain, with his mother, Maria Cristina

as regent. For almost a century, ever since the Napoleonic wars, Spain had been a battlefield of civil war and foreign intervention. The façade of constitutional monarchy was a means of keeping civil peace and holding down the fiery Spanish political temper. With clockwork regularity, conservatives and liberals alternated at the head of the govern-

An anti-American demonstration in Barcelona, Spain, in 1896

ment in Madrid. But the entire camouflage of parliament, regency, and cabinet rule could barely hide the fact that Spain was actually still being run as a giant feudal estate—and a feudal estate on the verge of bankruptcy. Peasants in Andalusia worked the great estates of absentee aristocrats under much the same conditions as during the middle ages; city workers were hardly better off. Anarchist, socialist, and republican groups were slaughtered from time to time by the police or the army—and it mattered little whether "conservatives" or "liberals" happened to be in office.

Like tottering regimes before and since, the Spanish monarchy insisted on past glories to divert popular attention from immediate problems. The island of Cuba—Spanish for four hundred years, since Columbus had first sailed west—was a symbol of that past glory. So too were the Philippines. In both colonies there were constant native insurrections—and in both colonies there were large colonial Spanish populations (today they would be called "*colons*") who were determined to maintain their exploitive grip on the natives. When, in the late 1890's, it became apparent that American imperialism had designs on both these Spanish possessions, the Spanish government had little choice but to fight. Giving up Cuba and the Philippines would mean revolt among the Spanish *colons* and even, possibly, revolt at home. Of course the Spanish government did everything it could to avoid war. American demands for autonomy for the Cubans and for the recall of harsh Spanish colonial officials were met. Up until the very last moment, even after American hysteria had been whipped up over the destruction of the *Maine*, the Spaniards sought to appease the United States. But American ambitions were not to be appeased—and when war came, the Spaniards resolved to fight—heroically, if helplessly—rather than submit to further degradation. Officials in Madrid were not completely without some dreams of success. On April 6, 1898, Admiral Beranger confided to the newspaper *Heraldo de Madrid:*

> "I have said before that we will win by sea and I'm going to give my reasons. The first is the enviable discipline that reigns aboard our warships. And the second is that when fire falls on the American ships they will disperse, since we all know that among their crews are to be found all nationalities."

Admiral Beranger was here referring to the fact that during the years of American naval decadence (1870–1888) American crews *were* recruited on a mercenary basis from any and all sources. But the admiral was out of date.

"I Have No Instructions . . ."

If Admiral Beranger, in the comfort of his office at the Ministry of Marine, could give optimistic interviews to the Madrid newspapers, Admiral Montojo, on the other side of the world, entertained no false hopes. From the day of his arrival at his new and unwanted command he had been raining cables on Madrid begging for supplies and instructions. Even as he left Madrid, Montojo asked for more ships. But the government promised to send him only the gunboats *Isla de Cuba* and *Isla de Luzon*—calling them "protected cruisers." When Montojo objected to such euphemism, he was informed that Admiral Beranger considered that the gunboats, because they had protected decks, were more useful than some larger ships might have been. And he was instructed not to worry, of all things, about war with Japan! But the admiral knew who and what he had to worry about.

When Montojo reached the Philippines he found his worst fears were well grounded. For the defense of this huge archipelago he had two cruisers, the *Reina Cristina* and the *Castilla*, and a collection of gunboats ranging in size from 500 tons to 1160 tons. In addition, guns were missing from some of these ships, and the *Castilla*'s engines were so ancient that they would no longer propel the ship—she had to be towed wherever she went. As for the mines and torpedoes which were supposed to protect the harbor mouth at Manila, they existed—but were so barnacle-encrusted, old-fashioned, and sparsely distributed as to be useless. True, there were heavy gun batteries placed on Corregidor, on El Fraile, and on the waterfront of the city of Manila—but few of these batteries had modern guns, their supply of ammunition was low, modern sighting and range-finding devices were non-existent, and the gunners had received little or no practice in recent years.

On March 15, 1898, having surveyed the hopelessness of his situation, Admiral Montojo called a council of war of his captains and aides. The admiral informed them that the United States squadron was assembling at Hong Kong, that the cruiser *Olympia*, with Dewey aboard, was there, and that the Americans must be getting ready to fight because they had sent their women to Shanghai and Yokohama. Furthermore, he had news that the huge and modern battleship *Oregon*, more than a match for all the Spanish ships in the Far East, was presently at Honolulu on her way to reinforce the already overwhelming American squadron. In this Montojo was mistaken—the ship on its way to Hong Kong was the cruiser *Baltimore*, with ammunition and supplies for Dewey. The only suggestion the assembled Spanish captains could make was that they ought to fight the Americans in

The United States cruiser Baltimore

Subic Bay. For supposedly there were shore batteries there and the bay could easily be protected by mines and torpedoes. From this sanctuary the Spanish ships might be able to make sudden dashes against the American squadron and perhaps damage a few of its ships. Montojo agreed and dispatched orders that Subic Bay be put in a state of preparedness.

But Montojo's efforts were like those of a man trying to struggle out of quicksand. On April 11th, General Arizmendi of the Spanish Army informed the admiral that shore batteries could not be emplaced at Subic until cement for their bases had been poured. But it seemed that Captain Rizzo of the engineers could not really say when cement would be ready or when it could be poured. Another officer of engineers, named Bacas, proposed making mines, but it was found that there was no nitroglycerine available. Montojo immediately cabled the Spanish Consul at Hong Kong asking for nitroglycerine—but received eight miles of electric cable instead! When Miguel Primo de Rivera, former Governor-General of the Philippines (who was on his happy way back to Madrid, having been replaced by General Basilio Augustin Davila) asked Montojo: "Don't you think the Americans might enter the bay and then bombard the city?" the weary admiral replied: "No—that would be a felony. But I don't have much confidence in their cordiality!"

And the struggle of the cables went on:

> MARCH 26, Montojo to Madrid: ". . . I have been actively taking all precautions. Torpedoes and boats few and deficient. I await superior orders. I have no instructions."

LEFT: *Patricio Montojo, commander of the Spanish Far Eastern fleet*

MARCH 27, Madrid to Montojo: ". . . approve all precautions taken in these circumstances regretting not being able to send reinforcements since they are needed here."

APRIL 11, Montojo to Madrid: ". . . they [the Americans] have more than fifty cannons. Mean speed seventeen knots. They will come as soon as war declared."

APRIL 12, Madrid to Montojo: ". . . hope your own zeal and activity will supplement deficiencies."

APRIL 19, Madrid to Montojo: ". . . shut island ports with defensive lines of torpedoes . . ."

APRIL 21, Montojo to Madrid: "Your Execellency knows that I have no torpedoes . . ."

APRIL 23, Montojo to Madrid: ". . . Before the immense superiority of the enemy's squadron of eight good ships against four deficient ones, I met with my captains and our majority opinion is to defend Subic Bay, leaving our squadron there in expectation of being able to take advantage of a favorable opportunity to defeat the enemy in detail or by surprise . . . I pray your Excellency answer me whether you approve or not."

APRIL 24, Madrid to Montojo: "Received your telegram dated yesterday."

Obviously the sacrificial victim was beginning to bore his superiors with all his clamor about guns and torpedoes and ships and such. All he and his men really had to do was to die and not run up the cable fees.

Fatalistically, the accustomed colonial life of Manila went on. The departing governor-general, Primo de Rivera, gave two balls—one at his palace at Malacañang, the other at Manila's Town Hall. Admiral Montojo gave a costume ball at his house in San Miguel. The Spanish Club of Manila gave a ball and presented the admiral with a sash decorated with precious stones.

At 11 P.M. on the 25th of April, Admiral Montojo, his flag aboard the cruiser *Reina Cristina*, led his forlorn assembly of ships to Subic Bay. The gunboats *Don Juan de Austria*, *Isla de Cuba*, and *Isla de Luzon*, the small dispatch boat *Marques del Duero*, and the old wooden cruiser *Castilla* followed after the flagship. The *Castilla*, which was little better than a floating battery, had to be towed—and even this comparatively gentle voyage put such a strain on her leaky hull that she began to ship water alarmingly. When he arrived at Subic, the admiral was disgusted, if not too surprised, to learn that almost nothing had come of the various plans to put the bay in a state of defense. Captain Del Rio, in charge of this matter, assured Montojo that the preparations would be completed "soon."

Since Subic was utterly undefended, Montojo could only hope that the Americans might not look into that bay, but proceed straight to Manila, thereby perhaps affording him enough time to complete Subic's defenses. This hope was shattered by a cable he received on April 28th informing him of the departure of Dewey's squadron for Subic Bay. A council of ship's captains was immediately convened—and they decided unanimously to return to Manila Bay and make a stand before the Naval Arsenal at Cavite. There, if the ships were sunk, the crews at least stood a good chance of making shore. Besides, the heavy shore batteries of Manila itself might add to the fleet's fire power. At 10 A.M. on April 29th—barely twenty-four hours before Dewey's ships entered Subic Bay—the Spanish fleet returned to Cavite. There the ships were spread into a line of battle before the Naval Arsenal, the *Castilla*'s hull filled with sand up to the water line to help protect her against shells—and the long wait began.

At 7 P.M. on April 30th, Montojo received word from Subic Bay that the Americans had looked in there and departed. At midnight gunfire was heard from the direction of Corregidor—and then silence. Montojo held a brief conference of his captains in the main cabin of the flagship *Reina Cristina*, advising them to scuttle their vessels rather than allow them to be captured. Then, accompanied by the *Reina Cristina*'s captain, Luis Cadarso, his own aide, Lieutenant Nuñez Quijano, and two steersmen, he climbed up to the *Reina Cristina*'s bridge to spend the next hours peering into the foggy night for his enemy. Perhaps he recalled then (with the disgust that a fighting man always entertains for civilian braggadocio) the unfortunate proclamation which had been issued by the pompous Governor-General Basilio Augustin Davila, just a week before.

"Spaniards!" the governor-general had proclaimed, ". . . A squadron manned by foreigners, possessing neither instruction nor discipline, is preparing to come to this archipelago with the ruffianly intention of robbing us of all that means life, honor, and liberty . . . Vain designs! Ridiculous boastings! . . . The aggressors shall not profane the tombs of your fathers, they shall not gratify their lustful passions at the cost of your wives' and daughters' honor, or appropriate the property your industry has accumulated as a provision for your old age . . ."

This proclamation had been read aboard all the American vessels as they steamed across the South China Sea—to the great amusement of the crews. Its effect on the Spanish sailors was simply one of irritation.

At 4:45 A.M. on May 1st, as the first light streaked the sky over Manila, Montojo ordered coffee served to his crews,

Basilio Augustin Davila, Governor-General of the Philippines

who'd been at battle stations for hours. And he spoke quite simply and directly to the crew of the *Reina Cristina:*

"Soldiers and sailors. The United States of America has obliged us to fight an iniquitous war when we could not have expected it. Its principal object is to rob us of the rich island which, for four hundred years, we have possessed by right of our discovery and conquest of the New World. But their ambition not satisfied with Cuba, they are coming to attack us also in this archipelago with a squadron far superior to our own. The enemy is in sight, and I am confident that all of you will demonstrate in combat that you are worthy companions of your forefathers in our country's history. Long live Spain! Long live the King!"

As the crew's cheers died away, a signal flag fluttered up the mast of the gunboat *Don Juan de Austria.* It was nearly 5 A.M. now, and through the harbor mist, the *Austria*'s captain, Juan de la Concha, had sighted the American squadron.

AMERICAN SQUADRON

Commodore George Dewey

Ship	Class	Tons	Guns	Crew	Captain
Olympia	Cruiser	5,870	4 8″, 10 5″ & 21 rapid-fire	381	C. V. Gridley
Baltimore	Cruiser	4,413	4 8″, 6 6″ & 8 rapid-fire	328	N. M. Dyer
Boston	Cruiser	3,000	2 8″, 6 6″ & 6 rapid-fire	230	F. Wildes
Raleigh	Cruiser	3,213	1 6″, 10 5″ & 12 rapid-fire	252	J. B. Coghlan
Concord	Gunboat	1,710	6 6″ & 6 rapid-fire	155	A. Walker
Petrel	Gunboat	892	4 6″ & 3 rapid-fire	110	E. P. Wood
McCulloch	Cutter	1,280	4 rapid-fire	68	D. B. Hodgson

RESUME: 7 ships: 20,378 tons: 109 guns (10 8″, 23 6″, 20 5″): 1,524 men

SPANISH SQUADRON

Rear Admiral Patricio Montojo y Pasarón

Ship	Class	Tons	Guns	Crew	Captain
Reina Cristina	Cruiser	3,520	6 6.2″ & 13 rapid-fire	352	L. Cadarso
Castilla	Cruiser	3,260	4 5″, 2 4.7″ & 14 rapid-fire	349	A. Algado
Isla de Cuba	Gunboat	1,045	4 4.7″ & 4 rapid-fire	156	L. Sidrach
Isla de Luzon	Gunboat	1,045	4 4.7″ & 4 rapid-fire	156	I. L. Human
Don Antonio de Ulloa	Gunboat	1,160	4 4.7″ & 6 rapid-fire	159	E. Robion
Don Juan de Austria	Gunboat	1,159	4 4.7″ & 8 rapid-fire	179	J. de la Concha
Marques del Duero	Cutter	500	1 6.2″, 2 4.7″	96	S. M. de Guerra

RESUME: 7 ships: 11,689 tons: 75 guns (7 6.2″, 4 5″, 20 4.7″): 1,447 men

NOTE. Spanish shore batteries around Manila included: 3 9.4″, 2 6.3″, 2 5.9″ and several 4.7″ guns.

3. "YOU MAY FIRE WHEN YOU ARE READY, GRIDLEY"

As the American squadron emerged from the misty dawn onto the placid waters of Manila Bay, a new chapter in the long history of naval warfare was about to commence. It is doubtful if the thought occurred to the tense gunners, the sweating coal stokers, or even to the tight-lipped commodore; but this would be the first fleet action in the world's history between steam-powered, steel ships. Individual steel ships had fought before—and during the Sino-Japanese War of 1894–1895, opposing fleets had clashed in a confused scramble which was more an assassination (of the Chinese fleet) than a battle. But the opening guns of Manila Bay were to herald a new era, which would last for the next four decades, during which the big guns of steel warships would rule the seas. On the morning of May 1, 1898, no one could be precisely sure what the results of an encounter between such fleets would be.

Commodore Dewey, and many of his officers, were old enough to have seen the revolution wrought in the world's navies by steam and steel. As young men they had trained and fought beneath billowing clouds of canvas on the decks of wooden warships not basically different from the warships of the preceding four centuries. Their ships were at the mercy of wind and current, and the winning captain in a sea fight was often the man who could turn these natural forces to his advantage. But in the years just preceding the American Civil War, steam power began to replace sails. During the war, high-velocity guns, firing explosive shells (as opposed to the old iron cannon balls) also made their appearance—and signaled the doom of wooden ships. The battle between the *Monitor* and the *Merrimac* in Hampton Roads, Virginia (and earlier battles between English and French warships pitted against Russian forts during the Crimean War), decisively demonstrated the superiority of the combination of steam and iron over sail and wood. But in the years of peace following the Civil War, an economy-minded Congress had refused to appropriate money to develop a new United States Navy. So U.S. naval officers, conscious that many of the most important inventions and developments of steam and steel navies had originated in their own service, were reduced to the humiliation of commanding a collection of wooden antiques which only inspired derision among foreign naval officers when the Americans made their yearly European and Asiatic cruises.

During the 1880's, under the impetus of reviving nationalism and the growing realization that American interests were rapidly becoming world-wide, a new American navy came into being. At first it was uncertain what form the new ships should take. Some of the earliest ships were built with spars to supplement steam power with sail power. Later it was found that no American companies were equipped to manufacture the necessary high-grade steel from which the new ships would have to be built. But, due almost entirely to the urgent demands of the Navy Department (and appropriations from Congress), American foundries quickly learned and mastered the skill of high-grade steel making—thereby establishing America's largest industry.

The new steel ships which began to emerge from American yards during the 1880's and 90's would be considered ridiculously small and inefficient today. Dewey's flagship, the *Olympia*, for example, would easily fit onto the flight deck of the modern aircraft carrier *John F. Kennedy*, and still leave plenty of room for planes to take off and land. Furthermore, the new ships generated steam by burning coal (oil-fired furnaces were still in their infancy)—and were therefore utterly dependent upon coaling stations. The imperialist practice of seizing islands and ports around the world in large part originated from the pressing need for places where

The USS Olympia, *flagship of Dewey's squadron*

huge dumps of coal could be stored to supply warships far from home.

To the men who sailed in them, the new ships were hard taskmasters. Coal was fed into the giant furnaces deep within the ships by muscle-power alone. Ventilation was poor, and temperatures below decks where the "black gangs" (so called because they were usually enveloped in a grimy mass of coal dust) labored often hovered around 110 degrees. In fact, the first casualty of the Battle of Manila Bay was chief engineer Frank Randall of the Coast Guard cutter *McCulloch* (whose soft-coal sparks had given away the squadron's presence off Corregidor during the night). Though some thought Randall died of mortification, he actually succumbed to heat prostration, and died before the squadron even entered Manila Bay.

Conditions were not much better for ships' gunners. Confined within small steel turrets where they served high-powered, rifled guns which shot explosive shells impelled by packs of gunpowder, the gunners lived during battle in a world of roaring explosions, stifling heat and lung-searing smoke. Furthermore, the combination of high-explosives, electricity, steam, and steel, was one relatively new to naval designers, architects, and builders. Safeguards against accidental explosion were rudimentary at best; turrets and entire ships had blown up with depressing frequency over the preceding twenty years. Range-finding devices by which guns could be trained and aimed were just beginning to be adopted. In fact, the American squadron was equipped with hastily rigged range-finders invented by Lieutenant Bradley Fiske, the young officer who had fallen asleep wondering whether the explosion of a mine off Corregidor would squash

him up against the deck of the *Petrel*. These new devices had never been tested in battle.

Nor were means of command very efficient on the new ships. Orders aboard ship were still transmitted orally by messengers, and between ships by signal flags hoisted on halyards. In actual practice, the transmission of a captain's order, by messenger to the officer commanding a gun turret,

A gun crew in action on an American warship

his shout to the gunners, their sighting of where their projectiles landed—all of this was not basically different from the means whereby John Paul Jones had commanded his ship more than a century before.

Traditionally, ships' captains in all the world's navies had always been individualists. Because of the impossibility of exactly coordinating ships' movements during the age of sail, fleets had always maneuvered more or less haphazardly. An admiral might indicate the broad outlines of an attack—but it was left to individual captains to carry out their instructions as best they could within very broad limits. Even Britain's great admiral, Horatio Nelson, at the Battle of Trafalgar had been able to indicate to his captains only how they could divide into squadrons, and generally, where and how they were to pierce the enemy's line of battle—after that he could state only that any ship laying herself alongside an enemy could not do wrong. And to the United States, which, more than any other naval power, had traditionally relied upon single-ship raids (and privateering) for defense at sea, and which had not maintained a navy large enough to be commanded in fleets and squadrons, the tradition of a captain's independence in battle was still strong. Since the 1880's, as enough of the new steel ships were commissioned, practice at maneuvering in squadrons had been incessant—but would the new system prove itself in battle? The American Asiatic squadron was, in many respects, a new and totally untried weapon in Commodore Dewey's hand.

All the uncertainties which plagued the American squadron were duplicated in the Spanish fleet. Admiral Montojo and his officers, who had taken their ships into action mostly against land fortifications during rebellions in Cuba and the Philippines or during the nineteeth century civil wars in Spain, had no more actual knowledge of what to expect than did the Americans. They were troubled by another problem which Dewey did not have to face. Since Spain had barely begun to industrialize at the end of the nineteenth century, most of the new Spanish steel warships were built abroad—in England or Italy or France—and purchased for their navy. Foreign naval architects often used such ships, which would never steam in their own country's line of battle, as a means of experimenting with new designs—often unworkable new designs. And, foreign ship yards often skimped on specifications, such as quality of steel and the small details of gun-training mechanisms or turret propulsion—which could be disastrous in actual battle.

But the doubts, uncertainties, and apprehensions which American and Spanish officers may have entertained about their fighting machines were swept away now in the mounting tension of approaching battle. Steel, steam, explosive shells, high-powered rifles, electricity—these might be ushering in a new age of naval warfare; but one ingredient of the new age would remain the same as it had over the centuries: the spirit of the men behind the guns.

"They Have Begun to Shoot at Us . . ."

At about 5 A.M. the American squadron swept into Manila Bay and headed for the city of Manila, searching for the Spanish fleet. Lieutenant Ellicott, cat napping between two eight-inch guns on the deck of *Baltimore*, was suddenly awakened by a shout from the bridge: "There they are!" Through the low-lying haze ahead, Ellicott could see a forest of masts and behind them the battlement and domes of Manila. But Captain Dyer, who was studying the scene through binoculars, said: "They are all merchant vessels." Ellicott pointed to starboard. "But look over there!" And there indeed was the Spanish fleet, a long line of dull gray ships stretching across Bacoor Bay in front of the Cavite Arsenal.

Admiral Montojo, fearful that a battle fought in front

ABOVE: *The* Olympia *leads the squadron into Manila Bay.* RIGHT: *The line of American ships closes in on the Spanish fleet.*

of Manila would expose the old city to stray shells from the American squadron, had elected to fight in the shallow waters before Cavite. In so doing he had to forgo the most effective support he might have expected from the heavy gun batteries placed before the city. As the American squadron held to its course, these batteries now opened fire, but their shells fell hopelessly short of the American ships.

Aboard the *Petrel*, Lieutenant Fiske, still asleep in his cabin, was awakened by a knock on the door and a voice calling: "The captain wishes to see you on the bridge." "What about?" Fiske replied sleepily. "I don't know," the voice said, "but it is ten minutes to five and they have begun to shoot at us." Fiske jumped from his berth and rushed to report to Captain Wood on the bridge. The captain simply smiled and said: "All right. The Spanish fleet is over there."

By this time Commodore Dewey had satisfied himself that no Spanish warships lurked before the city of Manila. The flagship *Olympia* swung 90 degrees to starboard and headed for the collection of ships waiting in front of Cavite. As the commodore glanced at the hills behind Manila he remarked to Captain Gridley that they reminded him of the blue hills of Vermont he'd known as a boy.

The American squadron proceeded in line-ahead formation, the *Olympia* first, followed in order by *Baltimore*, *Raleigh*, *Petrel*, *Concord*, and *Boston*. Each ship was separated from the vessel in front by about two hundred yards. The

transports *Nanshan* and *Zafiro* had already been ordered to another part of the bay under the protection of the little Coast Guard cutter *McCulloch*. Steadily and grimly, ignoring the wild shots which screamed over the men's heads from the Manila shore batteries, the little squadron bore down on the line of ships before Cavite.

The Spanish fleet waited motionless—the flagship *Reina Cristina* and the cruiser *Castilla* in the middle, with the gunboats *Don Juan de Austria*, *Don Antonio de Ulloa*, *Isla de Cuba*, and *Isla de Luzon*, and the cutter *Marques del Duero* stretched out on either side of the larger ships. They had steam up in their boilers, and their anchors were ready for slipping—but they did not emerge from the shallow waters of Bacoor Bay. At 5:15 A.M. Admiral Montojo opened fire on the approaching American squadron.

Juan Redondo, first medical officer of the Spanish fleet,

"The Battle of Manila Bay" by Gilbert Gaul

was busily sorting his shiny steel instruments below decks on the gunboat *Isla de Cuba* when he heard the roar and felt his ship rock to the firing of her guns. Redondo had carefully prepared the main cabin of the *Isla de Cuba* for its expected harvest of death—the iodine and bandages and antiseptics were all laid out in neat rows on a shiny nickel table. The doctor was satisfied with the cleanliness and efficiency of his "hospital"—but worried because *Isla de Cuba*'s passageways and hatch wells were so narrow that wounded men could only be conveyed through them carried in someone's arms. The sound of the guns aroused Redondo's curiosity and he clambered up on deck. A storm of firing now burst from the entire Spanish fleet—but still the American squadron kept silently and grimly on its course toward them.

As the Spanish ships opened fire Commodore Dewey signaled "Prepare for general action." Immediately huge

American battle flags broke out from the mastheads of the squadron. At the same time Lieutenant Ellicott could see the red and gold banners of Spain flutter to the mastheads of the fleet ahead. Captain Dyer, glancing up at the *Baltimore*'s battle flag, said to the men around him on the bridge: "Well, men, we have empty stomachs but full hearts. Let us see what can be done under the old flag once more." Lieutenant Ellicott later reflected that it seemed almost a sacrilege to cause those beautiful Spanish battle flags, emblems of four centuries of heroic history, to flutter down in defeat.

The Spanish fleet was now firing rapidly, but with little accuracy. Shells whistled over the American ships and splashed in the water all around them. Lieutenant Fiske had climbed up to his post atop the foremast of the *Petrel* to take range sightings on the Spanish fleet with the stadimeter he had invented. A Spanish shell suddenly exploded in the water so close to the *Petrel* that a great wave drenched Fiske in his post forty-five feet above deck. Tension mounted rapidly as the gunners of the American squadron waited in their turrets for the range to close. For twenty minutes they endured the rain of shells without replying.

On the *Olympia*'s bridge correspondent Stickney ducked as a Spanish shell burst directly over the ship. Commodore Dewey turned to Lieutenant Reese, the *Olympia*'s executive officer, and remarked: "About five thousand yards, I should say, eh Reese?" "Between that and six thousand, I should think, sir," the lieutenant replied. Dewey nodded, leaned over the bridge railing, and called down to the *Olympia*'s captain, who was stationed in the armored conning tower below: "You may fire when you are ready, Gridley."

LEFT: *Admiral Dewey on the bridge of the* Olympia

"From the boatswain's mate at the after five-inch gun," Stickney later recalled, "came a hoarse cry. 'REMEMBER THE MAINE!' arose from the throats of five hundred men at the guns . . ." At 5:41 A.M. the big eight-inch gun in the *Olympia*'s forward turret roared—and the American squadron opened fire. The big guns of the *Boston*, the *Raleigh*, and the *Baltimore* began to dispatch 250-pound high explosive shells to the Spanish fleet.

The Spanish shells were coming faster now. One missed the *Olympia*'s bridge by one hundred feet; another struck the bridge gratings, a third passed just under Commodore Dewey and gouged a hole in the deck. Aboard the *Boston*, paymaster Martin watched with horror as a Spanish shell passed through the ship's wardroom within five feet of his head—and failed to explode. Within the American turrets, as men sweated in a temperature of 116 degrees, their feet blistering against the hot steel decks, their cotton-stuffed ears aching from the roar of their own guns, firing continued as methodically as if they were at target practice.

"Cast loose and provide!" the turret officer would cry.

"Load!" Hundred-pound charges of powder followed 250-pound shells into the gun breeches.

"Point!" The trainers spun their geared wheels, trying to follow the fall of previous shots.

"Fire!" The ship rocked and the men were deafened as their gun spoke.

"Sponge!" The long-handled sponge steamed into the smoking gun breeches.

"Load!" and the smoke of gunpowder choked into the lungs of the gunners, blackened their faces, and blinded their eyes. Gunner Joel Evans, aboard the *Boston*, recalled: "Only the love of the work kept us going."

And if the men in the turrets were in purgatory, the stokers at the ship's furnaces were in hell. Down there the temperature reached two hundred degrees. Stoker Charles Twitchell, aboard the *Olympia*, recalled: "The battle hatches were all battened down, and we were shut in this little hole . . . it was so hot our hair was singed . . . the clatter of the engines and the roaring of the furnaces made such a din it seemed one's head would burst . . . the soot and cinders poured down on us in clouds . . . three of our men were overcome by the terrible heat . . ."

The American squadron ran down its distance to the Spanish fleet until it reached the five-fathom line of water

The Olympia *opens fire on the Spanish ships.*

Stokers feeding coal into the furnaces of a warship

depth before Cavite, then it turned to starboard to pass before the firing Spanish ships. Lieutenant Ellicott watched from the *Baltimore*'s bridge as "the American squadron stood past the Spanish ships and batteries in perfect column at six knots speed, making a run of two-and-a-half miles, then returned with starboard guns bearing. The first lap followed the five-fathom line as marked on the charts, and each succeeding one was made a little nearer, as soundings showed deeper water than the chart indicated." The stately parade of the American ships back and forth before the Spanish fleet gradually closed the range from three miles to one mile. The smoke of battle was so intense that it was not possible to judge accurately how much, if any, damage the heavy and rapid American firing was inflicting.

Aboard the Spanish ships, however, matters were dreadfully clear. A shell had gone through the *Cristina*'s forward turret, killing all the gunners there. The *Castilla*'s forward 4.5-inch gun was destroyed by a shell that went right down the barrel; a few minutes later the ship's secondary battery was knocked out. The *Isla de Luzon* had three of her guns dismounted and the little cutter *Marques del Duero* lost its prow gun. Only *Isla de Cuba* had not been seriously hit. The Spanish fleet was now a scene of horror. Fires had broken out on many of the ships, the screams of the wounded and dying mingled with the roar of terrible explosions as American shells continually found their marks. The *Cristina*, as the Spanish flagship, received a terribly concentrated fire. In the cruiser's main cabin, Dr. Antonio Siñiga worked desperately to treat the hordes of wounded who descended from the dead turrets. Suddenly an American shell burst right in the middle of the *Cristina*'s infirmary, setting it afire and dealing Siñiga a mortal wound.

Lieutenant Ellicott, aboard the *Baltimore*, watched admiringly as the burning and shell-riddled *Cristina* made a dash toward the American squadron "as if unable to longer endure her constricted position . . . but she turned away like a steed bewildered in a storm. It was then seen that she was on fire forward. Then a six-inch shell tore a jagged hole under her stern from which the smoke of another fire began to seep out. Right into the gaping wound another huge shell plunged, driving a fierce gust of flame and smoke out through her ports and skylights . . ."

A lifeboat pulls away from the devastated Reina Cristina.

Admiral Montojo ordered the *Cristina*'s hand rudder engaged as her steering motor was knocked out by the shell into her stern. The admiral was already wounded in the left leg by a shell fragment. The *Cristina*'s captain, Luis Cadarso had also been wounded. By this time the *Cristina*'s fires could no longer be controlled; half her crew was dead or wounded, and the afflicted vessel was heading erratically around toward the Cavite shore. Still her remaining two small rapid-fire guns spoke against the American ships—fired by two Marine corporals and loaded by deckhands and ship's stokers who'd replaced the dead gunners. But Montojo could no longer command his fleet from the crippled cruiser. He signaled the relatively unhurt *Isla de Cuba* that he was coming aboard, and climbed down into a launch floating near the *Cristina*. Meanwhile Captain Cadarso was attempting to transfer survivors from the *Cristina*'s crew to lifeboats when an American shell landed near-by, killing him instantly.

As the Americans saw Admiral Montojo's flag hoisted aboard the *Isla de Cuba* they shifted their fire from the beached and burning *Cristina* to the little gunboat. But still the *Cuba* remained unhurt. Below decks, Dr. Juan Redondo was now overwhelmed by wounded coming aboard from the *Cristina* with the admiral. None of them, the doctor later recalled, asked to have their wounds tended to—they only begged for water. Redondo was removing a large piece of shrapnel from a boatswain's arm when he was called to the bridge to treat Montojo. "I can't abandon this man whose life is in my hands!" the doctor exclaimed angrily. "Tell the admiral I'm coming right away!"

If the *Isla de Cuba* remained lucky, the *Castilla* did not. With only one of her stern guns still able to fire, the old wooden cruiser was ablaze from end to end. Her captain, Juan de la Concha, pacing grimly back and forth on her battered bridge looked to one observer like a man peering from the balcony of a ruined and burning house. The *Castilla*'s doctor, Manuel Ballesteros, had been wounded in the leg. As he lay on deck being treated by a medical orderly he was told that two stokers were bleeding to death on the ship's prow. Dr. Ballesteros had himself carried in the arms of two strong gunners over the burning deck to where the stokers lay, and there the wounded doctor treated the wounded men.

It was now 7:30 A.M.—barely two hours since the battle had started. Through the smoke, men and officers on the American ships could see that the *Cristina* was beached, the *Castilla* on fire and out of action, the *Isla de Luzon* burning fore and aft, and the *Marques de Duero* trying to make shore behind the Cavite Arsenal before she sank. But suddenly from the flagship *Olympia* came the signal, "Withdraw from action." Aboard the *Baltimore* officers and crew were dumbfounded. "Just as we were tearing them to pieces!" a seaman complained. Then another flutter of flags from the *Olympia*'s signal mast—"Let the men go to breakfast." Lieutenant Ellicott wondered why Dewey's signals were not in secret code. "Ha!" said Captain Dyer, "so's the enemy can read it. Who but Dewey would have thought of that!" The *Baltimore* followed the stately line of ships out to the middle of Manila Bay and Captain Dyer prepared to join his fellow captains aboard the *Olympia* for a council of war. As he left his ship, the *Baltimore*'s chaplain, who had spoken so fearfully of battle to Lieutenant Ellicott the night before, cried out: "We've got 'em! We've got 'em! Why don't we go in and finish 'em up?" Lieutenant Ellicott said quietly,

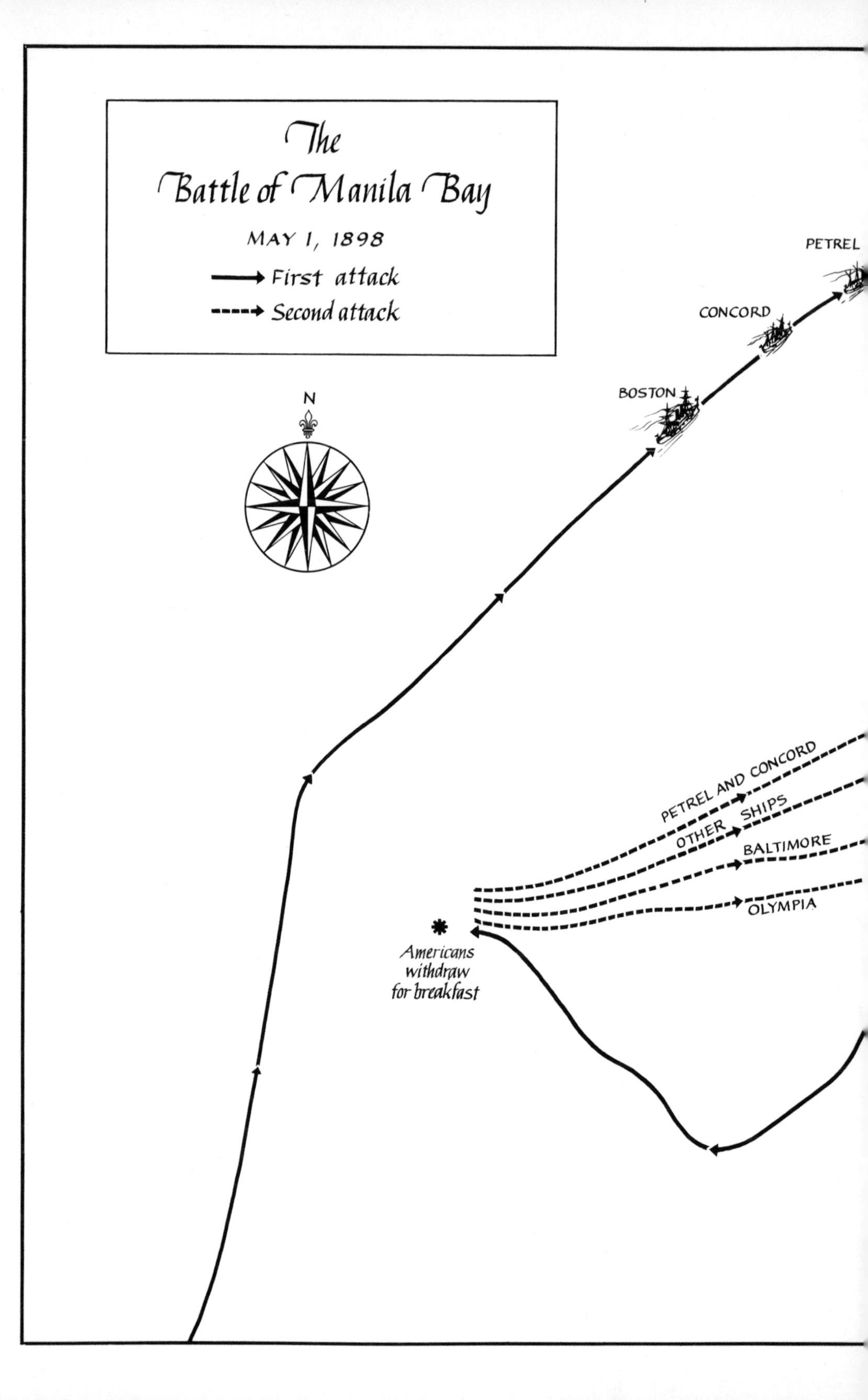
The
Battle of Manila Bay
MAY 1, 1898
First attack
Second attack
N
PETREL
CONCORD
BOSTON
PETREL AND CONCORD
OTHER SHIPS
BALTIMORE
OLYMPIA
Americans
withdraw
for breakfast

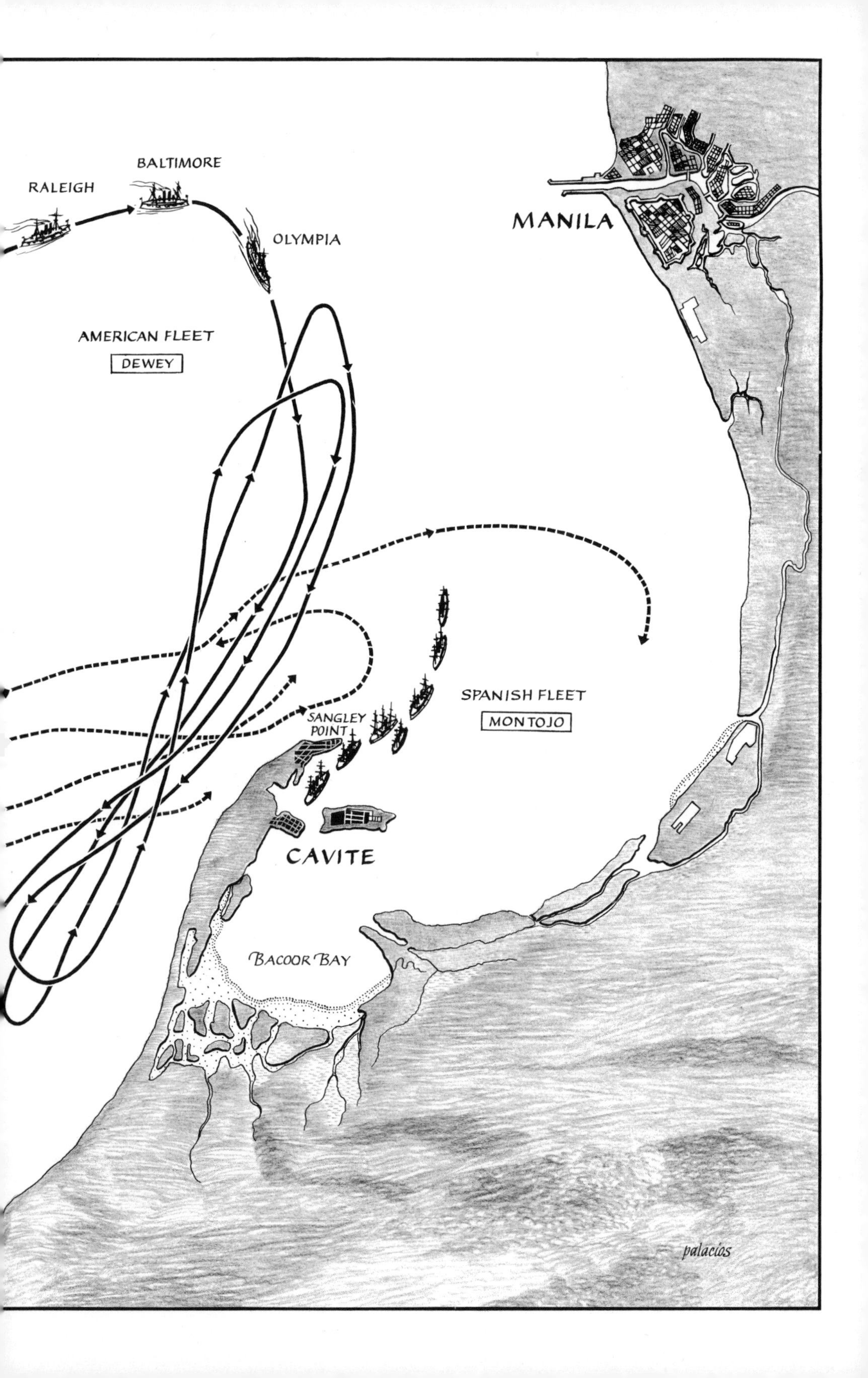
MANILA
BALTIMORE
RALEIGH
OLYMPIA
AMERICAN FLEET
DEWEY
SPANISH FLEET
MONTOJO
SANGLEY POINT
CAVITE
BACOOR BAY
palacios

The Reina Cristina *after the battle*

"You forget, chaplain. Over *there* are the scenes you pictured last night." The chaplain's eyes filled with tears and he went below.

As the American captains assembled aboard the *Olympia* they were amazed to find that none of them had either serious damage or any deaths to report. Not a single American had died during the battle. Aboard the *Baltimore* two officers and six enlisted men had been slightly wounded—and they were the only casualties! The few Spanish shells which had found their mark had had little effect on the American ships.

The captains also learned that Dewey had ordered them to break off the action because he had been informed that the *Olympia* had only a few rounds of 5-inch ammunition left. But it was now discovered that this report was an error. All the ships had sufficient ammunition to continue battle.

However, the battle was all but over. While Dr. Redondo treated Admiral Montojo's wound on the bridge of the *Isla de Cuba*, the admiral was dictating a telegram to Governor-General Augustin Davila announcing the total defeat of his fleet. Then the admiral ordered that those of his ships remaining afloat be scuttled and abandoned, if the Americans renewed their attack. Followed by his officers, the admiral went ashore at 10 A.M. and made his way to Cavite Arsenal, where the arsenal's commander, Captain Enrique Sostoa, congratulated him on his gallant fight. It was from the arsenal that Admiral Montojo sadly watched the American squadron steam back to its attack at 11:05 A.M.

By now the Americans could see that of the Spanish ships still afloat, the *Isla de Cuba* and the *Marques del Duero* had retired behind the breakwater of the Cavite Arsenal. Only the gunboat *Don Antonio de Ulloa* remained at the tip of Sangley Point to offer continued resistance. The *Baltimore* was ordered to silence the shore batteries of Cavite, and this she did in a short but savage duel, the big cruiser steaming slowly back and forth, placing shot after shot into the em-

The wreck of the cruiser Don Antonio de Ulloa

bankments ashore. Meanwhile the entire fire of the American squadron was concentrated on the *Ulloa*. Riddled with shells, burning fore and aft, the gallant little gunboat continued her hopeless duel until, her guns all dismounted, her crew leaping into the water, she rolled over and sank. By this time the Spanish flags over the gun batteries ashore had been hauled down and replaced by white flags. Only the Cavite Arsenal still displayed the proud banner of Spain. Because of her light draft, the gunboat *Petrel* was ordered to enter the waters just in front of the arsenal and burn any Spanish ships still floating there. This the *Petrel* accomplished with dispatch, the Spaniards offering no resistance. The gunboat fired a few shots—and the flag over the arsenal came fluttering down. Commodore Dewey, satisfied that the Spaniards had finally surrendered, turned the *Olympia* back toward Manila. The big cruiser, followed by the rest of the squadron, anchored peacefully off the city at 1:30 P.M.

Dewey had destroyed seven Spanish warships—the entire effective force of the Spanish Far Eastern fleet—killed or wounded nearly four hundred enemy officers and men, and was now undisputed master of Manila Bay. All this had been accomplished at a cost of a few slightly wounded men and no more damage to American ships than the men could easily repair afloat. That evening, as the lights of Manila twinkled in the distance, the commodore enjoyed his traditional nightly band concert aboard the *Olympia*. In honor of the occasion, the ship's band played the commodore's favorite march: "Under the Double Eagle." For the benefit of the throngs of Spaniards and Filipinos who crowded down to the waterfront to stare in awe at the grim American fighting ships, the *Olympia*'s band played "La Paloma."

4. TO THE VICTOR...

While the band concert on the evening of May 1st may have signaled the end of a battle to the listening crews and the population of Manila, to Commodore Dewey it merely marked the end of the first phase of a campaign. He had destroyed his enemy's sea power in the Far East—but he had not conquered the city of Manila, let alone the vast Philippine archipelago. His ammunition was now depleted and he was still thousands of miles from supplies or an American base. He had neither the men nor the means to capture Manila and convert that port into a base—and although his squadron ruled the waters of the bay, the troops of Governor-General Augustin Davila continued in firm control of the city. An uneasy truce—a balance of bluff—had already been established between the commodore and the pompous governor-general.

Governor-General Davila, commandant of Manila, with his officers

Immediately following the battle, while Dewey's flagship, the *Olympia*, was steaming to her anchorage before Manila, the commodore had sent word to Augustin Davila through the British Consul in Manila, that if the governor-general's heavy shore batteries remained silent, the American squadron would refrain from bombarding the city. To this proposal Davila eagerly agreed. But to Dewey's further suggestion—that the underwater cable which was Manila's sole telegraphic link with the outside world be shared on equal terms by the American squadron and the Spanish authorities—the governor-general turned a deaf ear. So while the strains of "La Paloma" floated soothingly over Manila Bay, the supply ship *Zafiro* quietly dredged up the cable and cut it. Augustin Davila's splendid isolation thus became complete.

Word of the American victory had, nevertheless, gotten through. And when Dewey's confirming dispatches (sent by steamer to Hong Kong and cabled from there) reached Washington, the American people went wild with joy. Torchlight parades were held in towns and villages throughout the country; state legislatures and Congress voted thanks and praise to the men of the Asiatic squadron; President McKinley immediately elevated Dewey to the rank of rear admiral; honorary medals and coins were ordered struck, garishly decorated presentation swords were prepared, and Dewey leaped overnight from obscurity to the pantheon of national heroes.

All this acclaim did not, however, solve any of Rear Admiral Dewey's very real problems. First there was the question of reinforcements. While Dewey had destroyed Spain's Far Eastern fleet (and in subsequent days spiked the heavy guns at Manila, Corregidor, and Cavite), he had by no means destroyed the Spanish Navy. And as his ships swung to their moorings beneath the tropical heat of the Manila sun, he knew that Spain would make some attempt to recapture command of Manila Bay. During the month of May, Dewey received a report that Spanish admiral Pascual Cervera was at sea in the Atlantic with a squadron of fast, heavy cruisers (much more than a match for the force under Dewey's command). While it was believed that Cervera's destination was Cuba, this was not certain. Then when Cervera *did* appear in Cuba late in May, still another Spanish fleet, under the command of Admiral Manuel de la Camara and including a powerful, if aged battleship, set sail in the Mediterranean heading east—and there could be no doubt that this one was on its way to Manila.

The U.S. Navy Department had already dispatched the cruiser *Charleston* to Manila with fresh supplies of ammunition. A week before Admiral Camara sailed the navy ordered the ancient (but heavily gunned) monitors *Monterey* and *Monadnock* to join the Asiatic squadron. These two vessels, of Civil War design, had never been intended for duty far from the mouth of a harbor. Their voyage across the Pacific was in itself an odyssey of courage and endurance—but before they arrived, the problem of Admiral Camara's fleet had been solved on the basis of a suggestion made by Admiral Dewey. He told the Navy Department that the surest way of forcing Camara to return to Spain was to send a powerful squadron to attack the Spanish coast. Accordingly, at the end of June, Washington let it be known that a heavy American fleet would soon carry the war to Spain's home waters. Within one week, Admiral Camara's fleet (which had already passed through the Suez Canal) was homeward bound.

Germany Makes an Enemy

It was not only fear of Spanish reinforcements which worried Dewey. He was also concerned about the very strange behavior of German warships in Manila Bay. Shortly after the battle, warships of several neutral nations had arrived at Manila. They were there, quite properly, to protect their countries' citizens, and also so that their officers could study the results of the battle. But under international maritime law

RIGHT: *The* Chicago Daily Tribune *the day after Dewey's victory*

The Chicago Daily Tribune.

THEY REMEMBERED THE MAINE!

VOLUME LVII.—NO. 122. MONDAY, MAY 2, 1898—TWELVE PAGES. PRICE

GREAT SEA VICTORY FOR AMERICA!

VENGEANCE FOR THE MAINE BEGUN!

SPAIN'S ASIATIC FLEET BURNED AND SUNK!

Washington Aflame with Joy Over the Reports of the Royal Victory Won by Commodore Dewey's Fleet.

NOTABLE COMPANY HEARS THE NEWS.

Additional Credence Lent to the Dispatches from Madrid Because They Emanated from Distinctively Spanish Sources.

THINK THE DEFEAT HAS BEEN DECISIVE.

General Rejoicing That the First Real Engagement of the War Should Have Been So Triumphant for the American Cause.

ENTHUSIASTIC COMMENT OF GUESTS OF PRESIDENT M'KINLEY.

HERO OF THE BATTLE OF MANILA.

COMMODORE GEORGE DEWEY,
Commander of the Victorious Asiatic Fleet of the American Navy.

KNOWN CASUALTIES OF THE FIGHT.

Spanish cruiser REINA MARIA CHRISTINA, Admiral's flagship, burned.

Spanish cruiser CASTILLA, said to be completely burned.

Spanish cruiser DON JUAN DE AUSTRIA, blown up.

Several Spanish ships sunk.

Cadarso, Captain of the Spanish flagship, and crew of 370, who perished with the vessel.

Commanders of the Spanish cruisers Castilla and Don Juan de Austria, with their crews of about 500 men all told.

American losses are unknown.

SUMMARY.

United States vessels lost (Madrid admission)	0
United States vessels damaged (from best information)	0
Spanish cruisers totally lost (Madrid admission)	3
Spanish gunboats damaged (Madrid admission)	2
Spanish Captains lost (commanding lost cruisers)	3

SHIPS THAT FOUGHT OFF MANILA.

UNITED STATES FLEET.

OLYMPIA (flagship), first-class cruiser, Capt. C. V. Gridley.
BALTIMORE, protected cruiser, Capt. N. M. Dyer.
BOSTON, protected cruiser, Capt. Frank Wildes.
RALEIGH, protected cruiser, Capt. J. B. Coghlan.
CONCORD, gunboat, Commander Asa Walker.
PETREL, gunboat, Commander E. P. Wood.
M'CULLOCH, dispatch boat.
NANSHAN, collier.
ZAFIRO, collier.

SPANISH FLEET.

REINA MERCEDES, cruiser.
REINA CRISTINA, cruiser.
ISLA DE CUBA, cruiser.
ISLA DE LUZON, cruiser.
CASTILLA, cruiser.
DON ANTONIO DE ULLOA, cruiser.
DON JUAN DE AUSTRIA, cruiser.
VELASCO, cruiser.
ELCANO, gunboat.
GENERAL LEZO, gunboat.
MARQUES DEL DUERO, gunboat.
QUIROS, gunboat.
VILLALOBOS, torpedo gunboat.
GENERAL ALAVA, transport.
CEBU, transport.
MANILA, transport.
ISLA DE MINDANAO, converted cruiser.

Commodore Dewey Crushes the Spanish Squadron in a Terrific Battle Off Cavite, Near the Capital of the Philippine Islands, Sunday Morning.

ONE OF THE GREAT NAVAL ENGAGEMENTS OF THE AGE.

Admiral Montejo's Flagship, the Reina Maria Christina, and the Cruiser Castilla Are Burned, While the Don Juan de Austria Is Blown Up.

OTHERS ARE SUNK TO SAVE THEM FROM BEING CAPTURED.

Captain Cadarso Is Among the Killed on the Spanish Side, and the List of Fatalities Is a Large One, Though the Particulars on This Point Are Slow in Coming to Hand.

LOSS TO AMERICA'S WARSHIPS AND SAILORS IS NOT BELIEVED TO BE HEAVY.

Commodore Dewey's squadron won a decisive victory over the Spanish fleet yesterday.

The battle was fought off Cavite, ten miles southwest of Manila. It lasted for several hours and resulted in a crushing defeat for Spain.

The American squadron arrived off the Philippines on Saturday night, taking advantage of the darkness to gain a favorable position. The attack on the Spanish fleet began soon after daylight yesterday morning.

It was a terrific battle, undoubtedly one of the fiercest and most brilliant in the history of naval warfare. The nine ships of the American fleet were outnumbered by those of Spain, but the Americans were superior in armament.

The heavy fire from Commodore Dewey's guns was effective from the outset. Admiral Montejo's flagship, the Reina Maria Christina, was burned and its commander killed. The Don Juan de Austria was blown up and the Castilla was burned.

The Spanish sailors fought bravely, and refused to leave their burning ships when ordered to do so. Commander Cadarso of the flagship went down with his vessel, and many of his crew perished with him.

Others of the Spanish fleet were badly damaged, and were sunk to prevent their falling into the hands of the Americans.

There was considerable loss of life on the Spanish side.

The American losses are not stated. As most of the news is sent by the Governor General of the Philippines it is certain that if Commodore Dewey's squadron was materially damaged the fact would not be minimized.

Admiral Montejo cabled to Madrid admitting the defeat of his squadron.

One Spanish report says that the American commander retired after an hour's fighting to land his wounded.

The battle took the form of a double engagement, according to the somewhat indefinite reports on this point. Presumably these reports are based on the manoeuvers of the American squadron. The statement is made that Commodore Dewey's ships withdrew for a time and then returned to the attack. As the advantage was all on his side from the first, it is not believed that he at any period in the fight withdrew from action, though his ships may have changed positions.

The news of the Spanish defeat was fully confirmed in Lisbon last night, where the early reports gave Spain the victory.

Madrid officials profess to consider the battle a brilliant page in the nation's history, and the Minister of Marine telegraphed praise and congratulations to Admiral Montejo.

The feeling in London is that Commodore Dewey's job cannot be considered complete until he has captured Manila, and that he will be in an awkward position unless he succeeds in taking the city.

There was wild enthusiasm in Washington when the news of the victory arrived.

REINA MARIA CHRISTINA, SPANISH FLAGSHIP, BURNED.

STORY OF THE BATTLE

Spain Admits the Disaster in Which Its Fleet Was Routed at Manila.

they were duty bound to accept the port rules and authority of the victorious American blockading squadron. This they all did—except the German ships. Also, the German squadron steadily increased in strength as ship after ship arrived during the month of May. The cruisers *Irene* and *Kaiserin Augusta* were joined by the *Prinzess Wilhelm,* the *Cormoran,* and others, until Vice Admiral von Diedrichs, the German commander, disposed of a much larger force than did Dewey. On a courtesy visit to the German admiral, Dewey asked why so large a force of German ships had gathered (there were few German "interests" to be guarded in the Philippines). Von Diedrichs clicked his heels together and proclaimed: "I am here by order of the Kaiser, sir!" That, evidently, should have been sufficient explanation for anyone.

Actually, as Dewey well understood, imperial Germany, now under the leadership of her fiery young Kaiser, Wilhelm II (whose ambitions would one day help bring about World War I), supported the cause of imperial Spain in the present conflict. More than that, it was well known that Germany was eager to acquire colonies in the Far East. Thus Admiral von Diedrichs' behavior might be no more than the usual Prussian bad manners—or it might be a deliberate policy to provoke Dewey into a rash action which would give Germany an excuse to seize the Philippines for herself.

And Von Diedrichs' behavior worsened daily. His ships sailed in and out of Manila Bay without bothering to report to the American blockading squadron, or even to acknowledge its signals; the Germans landed marines and set up a small "base" on the mainland of Luzon opposite Corregidor; they displayed ostentatious signs of good will and approval

The Irene *and other ships of Admiral von Diedrichs' squadron*

to the Spanish forces ashore, carried messages for them, and sent them "presents" of food and wine from ships' stores. Worst of all, they finally even began to interfere in the insurrectionary war between Filipino rebels and Spanish troops which had flared into new life with the American victory. By the beginning of June Admiral Dewey's patience was at an end.

On June 8th, a young German staff officer, sent by Admiral von Diedrichs to protest American harbor rules, was asked by Dewey: "Does His Excellency know that it is my force and not his which is blockading this port?"

"Yes, sir," the German replied.

"And is he aware that he has no rights here except those I choose to allow him?"

The German shrugged.

"One would imagine, sir, that you were conducting this blockade."

The German shrugged again.

"Do you want war with us?" Dewey demanded suddenly.

"Certainly not," the German replied nervously.

"Well," Dewey declared, his voice rising to a shout that could be heard throughout the ship, "it looks like it, and you are very near it, and you can have it, sir, as soon as you like!"

The German officer returned in consternation to Vice Admiral von Diedrichs with this chilling bit of information. Von Diedrichs, thoroughly alarmed, asked the commander of the small British squadron, Captain Chichester, what he thought of the matter. Chichester, an admirer and friend of Dewey's, was under instructions from his British government to cooperate with the Americans in every possible way. He calmly informed the German admiral that Commodore

Dewey was well within his rights—and definitely not to be trifled with. From Captain Chichester's tone and manner, Von Diedrichs concluded that if a fight broke out between his ships and the American squadron, Dewey would not find himself fighting alone. Thereafter, German provocation ceased in Manila Bay, though Von Diedrichs' squadron remained. Nothing was really settled yet—nothing could be settled, until the Americans either captured Manila or decided to withdraw. And this was by no means a simple decision.

The Capture of Manila

Before he left Hong Kong, Dewey had been in touch with the leader of the Filipino insurrectionists, Emilio Aguinaldo. This fiery young revolutionary had risen to leadership of the latest of the Filipino rebellions against Spanish rule, just two years before. Driven from the islands in 1896 by the military skill of Governor-General Primo de Rivera, Aguinaldo had continued to direct underground resistance secretly from Hong Kong. With the opening of the Spanish-American War, largely because the United States proclaimed its sole intent to be the liberation of the oppressed natives of another island, Cuba, Filipino insurrectionists thought their day of freedom had naturally dawned too. There is no doubt at all that both the American Consul at Hong Kong and Dewey himself encouraged Aguinaldo in this belief. Nor is there any doubt that Dewey, for one, suspected that the United States might be misleading the Filipino leader. Nevertheless, encouragement of the Filipino rebels was considered a necessary war measure.

Dewey sent for Aguinaldo and thirteen of his staff, who came over from Hong Kong aboard the *Nanshan* on May 19th. The rebels with little or no American aid quickly established headquarters near Cavite Arsenal and by June 15th they had captured 2,500 Spaniards, had occupied all the area around Cavite, and were besieging the city of Manila itself. On May 24th, Aguinaldo proclaimed: ". . . the great and powerful North American nation has come to offer disinterested protection for the effort to secure the liberation of this country." But had Aguinaldo known what decisions had already been reached in Washington, he would not have rejoiced.

Later, President McKinley was to describe to a group of clergymen how he "walked the floor of the White House night after night . . . and I am not ashamed to tell you, gentlemen, that I went down on my knees and prayed Almighty God for light and guidance . . ." But in fact, on May 3, even before Dewey's official report confirming his victory arrived in Washington, McKinley accepted the suggestion of Commanding General of the Army Nelson Miles that troops be sent to Manila. This could only mean to Miles landing to seize the city—and that could only mean McKinley planned to retain an American naval base, at least, after the war and, probably, to retain the entire archipelago. This was the original hope and plan of Assistant Secretary of the Navy Theodore Roosevelt, and was certainly a plan which Dewey heartily endorsed.

The American troops under Major General Wesley Merritt, the expeditionary force's commander, who sailed from

LEFT: *Emilio Aguinaldo, leader of the Filipino insurrectionists*

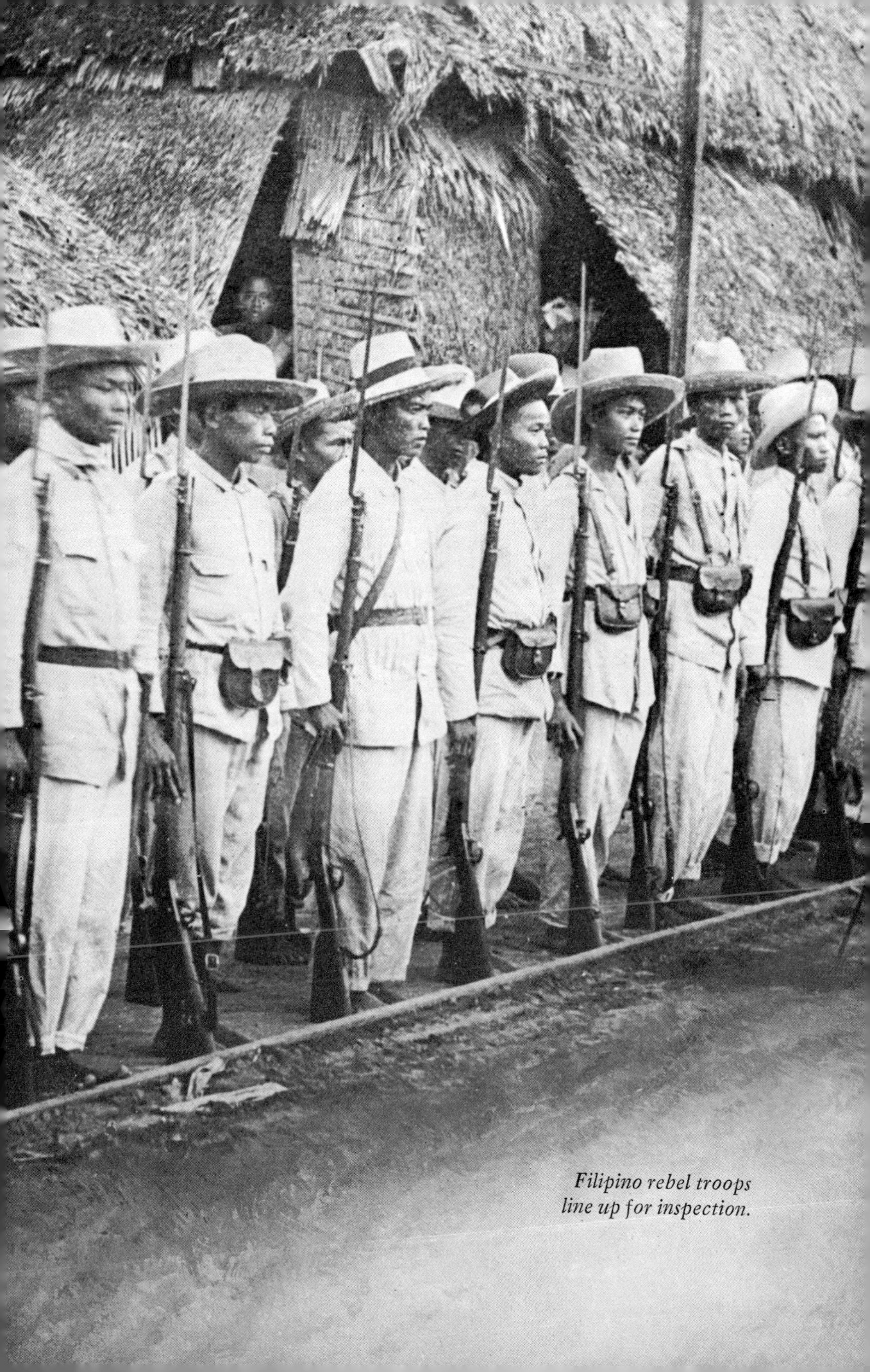

Filipino rebel troops line up for inspection.

San Francisco on May 25th, convoyed by the cruiser *Charleston*, arrived at Manila Bay on June 30th. On the way the expedition had captured the island of Guam (the Spaniards there did not even know they were supposed to be at war). Further contingents of troops arrived until the Americans numbered about ten thousand—including Brigadier General Arthur MacArthur, father of a youngster at West Point who would one day make a name for himself in the Philippines.

August 13: American troops signal their position to the Navy.

Admiral Dewey had already conceived of the possibility that Manila might be taken without a real battle. The Spaniards there, under their new governor-general, Fermin Jaudenes (the hapless Augustin Davila had been relieved), were much more frightened at the prospect of Aguinaldo's Filipino rebels capturing Manila than at the thought of American occupation. To preserve "face" at home, the Manila garrison could not surrender outright—but Jaudenes had already indicated to Dewey that he would offer no

ABOVE: *The First Colorado Regiment advancing toward Manila*
RIGHT: *General Arthur MacArthur's headquarters on August 13th*

serious opposition to an American attempt to seize Manila. Secret negotiations between Jaudenes and Dewey and Merritt were carried on through the long hot weeks of July and into August, while the men of the expeditionary force sweated in their shallow trenches ashore, exchanging occasional gunfire with distant Spanish outposts, getting in the way of Aguinaldo's men, and succumbing to tropical heat and yellow fever.

On August 13th, Merritt and Dewey undertook one of the strangest battles in military history. It was carefully designed to *prevent* bloodshed, but preserve honor. First (to their growing suspicion), Aguinaldo and his men were herded out of the way and American troops took over their lines outside Manila. Then, at 8:45 A.M. Admiral Dewey's squadron, reinforced now by the cruiser *Charleston* and the monitors *Monterey* and *Monadnock*, battle flags unfurled, steamed in line, the *Olympia* leading the way, toward the Manila batteries. As the proud squadron passed Captain Chichester's British ships, the *Immortalité* and the *Iphigenia*, the British seamen cheered and their bands played Dewey's favorite: "Under the Double Eagle." Then, as the American squadron moved on, the British ships steamed slowly away until they had placed themselves squarely between Von Diedrichs' German squadron and the Americans. The gesture was not lost upon Von Diedrichs or upon the grateful Americans.

At 9:35 A.M. the American ships began a slow and careful bombardment of Fort San Augustin, two miles from Manila.

There was no answering Spanish fire and, from the ships, the lines of running, cheering American troops ashore could be seen steadily advancing upon the fort. They swarmed over it at 10:35 A.M. and hoisted the Stars and Stripes. Meanwhile, Dewey, aboard *Olympia*, had ordered the international signal "D.W.H.B." hoisted to the signal masthead. It meant "Surrender!" And, by pre-arrangement with Governor-General Jaudenes, it was to be answered by a white flag. At 11:20 A.M. the Spaniards' white flag was seen on the city walls, and Dewey sent a group of officers ashore. They were met by Governor-General Jaudenes and by Admiral Montojo. By 2:00 P.M. the Spanish officials had agreed to articles of capitulation. Even while surrender terms were being discussed, American troops were entering the city. At 5:43 P.M., the men of Dewey's squadron were thrilled to see a giant American flag break out over the Spanish citadel in the heart of Manila, and hear the echoing strains of a regimental band playing "The Star-Spangled Banner"—immediately, the heavy ships of the squadron roared out a 101-gun national salute. Manila had fallen. Because the cable had not been repaired, no one in the Philippines knew that on the other side of the world, in Paris, the day before (Friday, August 12th) an armistice had been signed between Spain and the United States.

CHRONOLOGY

FEBRUARY 15, 1898. United States Battleship *Maine* blows up in Havana harbor.

FEBRUARY 25. Admiral George Dewey receives orders to prepare the United States Asiatic fleet for war.

MARCH 15. Admiral Patricio Montojo, Commander of the Spanish fleet in the Philippines, holds a council of war which decides to meet the American squadron in Subic Bay on the west coast of Luzon.

APRIL 22. The American cruiser *Baltimore*, with ammunition, joins Dewey's squadron at Hong Kong.

APRIL 23. The United States declares war on Spain.

APRIL 25. Dewey's squadron leaves Hong Kong harbor. Montojo's squadron arrives at Subic Bay. Montojo finds that his orders to put the bay in a state of defense have not been carried out.

APRIL 28. Montojo learns that Dewey has left Hong Kong. Dewey's destination: Subic Bay.

APRIL 29. Montojo leaves Subic Bay to offer battle in Manila Bay before Cavite.

APRIL 30. The American squadron looks into Subic Bay. Not finding the Spanish fleet, it departs.

APRIL 30–MAY 1, midnight. Dewey's ships slip past the fortified islands of Corregidor and El Fraile. The Spanish batteries on El Fraile open up. The American ships return the fire, silencing the enemy's guns with a few shots.

MAY 1, 2:00 A.M. Dewey's squadron reduces speed to four knots in order to arrive off Manila in daylight.

5:00 A.M. The United States squadron swings past Manila, is

sighted by Montojo, and draws desultory fire from the Manila shore batteries.

5:15 A.M. Spanish ships open fire on the American squadron.

5:40 A.M. American ships open fire on the Spanish fleet.

7:30 A.M. Dewey's ships pull away for breakfast and a casualty report.

10:00 A.M. Montojo, wounded, goes ashore at Cavite. Most of his fleet is sunk.

11:05 A.M. American ships renew their attack.

12:45 P.M. Spaniards surrender Cavite Arsenal in the face of American bombardment. All Spanish ships are sunk or captured.

1:30 P.M. Dewey's squadron anchors off the city of Manila.

MAY 3. President William McKinley orders dispatch of American Expeditionary Force to the Philippines.

MAY 19. Dewey brings Filipino rebel leader Emilo Aguinaldo and thirteen of his staff to the Philippines from Hong Kong.

MAY 25. The American Expeditionary Force sails from San Francisco.

JUNE 7. Admiral Manuel de la Camara sets sail from Spain with a new squadron for the Far East.

JUNE 14. United States monitors *Monterey* and *Monadnock* depart from San Francisco for Manila.

JUNE 28. Admiral Camera turns back for Spain on receiving a report than an American fleet is being organized to attack the Spanish coast.

JUNE 30. The American Expeditionary Force arrives at Manila.

JULY 3. The Spanish Atlantic squadron is sunk off Santiago de Cuba.

AUGUST 12. An armistice between Spain and the United States is signed in Paris.

AUGUST 13. The American Expeditionary Force, supported by Dewey's squadron, seizes Manila after a prearranged "face-saving" battle with the Spanish forces of Governor-General Fermin Jaudenes.

5. THE SANDS OF TIME

And so the Manila campaign ended. It had been marked throughout by the brilliance of one man—George Dewey, who had thoroughly prepared himself, his men, and his ships for a task which many thought to be impossible, and then carried it through with coolness, daring, and grim attention to detail. The running of the land batteries and mine fields of Corregidor at night had been carried out with an aplomb and indifference to danger of which Dewey's old commander, Admiral Farragut, would have been proud. The battle itself was a masterpiece of careful concentration of force to achieve a desired objective. There have been larger sea battles fought, before and since Manila Bay; but few have ended in as complete a victory. Dewey's combination of firmness and diplomacy during the weeks after the battle while he awaited reinforcements from home did much to

SINGER
PARA COSER
BIOGRAPH

enhance American prestige throughout the world; his careful plan for the bloodless capture of Manila itself saved countless American and Spanish lives. As a French admiral remarked to Dewey after Manila fell: "Admiral, you must let me congratulate you that in all your conduct of affairs here you have not made a single mistake." Characteristically, Dewey replied: "Oh, yes I have. I made one—I should have sunk that squadron over there," pointing to Admiral von Diedrichs' ships. The French admiral smiled appreciatively.

The consequences of the Battle of Manila Bay were mostly hidden from the participants by the misty horizons of time. But a keen-eyed observer might have noted the new ties of friendship between British and American naval men, and the definite planting of seeds of hostility against the naval power of imperial Germany. Perhaps such an observer could have begun to see the outlines of that world-wide Anglo-American alliance which would one day fight imperial Germany. An observer would have had no trouble at all in foreseeing the long, bloody, and bitter war which was now to break out between the United States and Emilio Aguinaldo's Filipino independence movement, and the fifty-year domination of the Philippines by the United States.

Japan had already begun to make imperialistic noises in Asia—could it be foreseen that by planting its forces athwart those routes of conquest which were already luring Japan's war lords, the United States had made an ultimate war with Japan all but certain? Americans soon realized that to retain possession of the Philippines, the United States would have to build the kind of navy which could defend its colonies

LEFT: *A street in Manila soon after the American occupation*

President McKinley and Admiral Dewey in front of the Capitol

against any and all comers. And that new navy (which within two decades was to be larger than any other except those of England and Germany) would need bases. Hawaii had been annexed during the summer of 1898, and Guam captured. With the fall of Manila the string of islands—Wake, Midway, Howland, and Baker—between Hawaii and the Philippines, all of which would figure in later battles in another war, were added to America's chain of bases—stepping stones to the Far East. The United States had staked out its claim as a great and interested power in Asian affairs—a claim which was to have consequences which are still unfolding.

If victory had its consequences, not all of them sweet, defeat had consequences which were not entirely bitter. Spain was relieved of its tremendously costly expenditure in trying to maintain a colony which had enriched a few Spaniards, but been an economic burden to the mass of the Spanish people. Although defeat in 1898 did not topple the Spanish monarchy, it jolted a considerable group of Spanish philosophers, writers, politicians, and artists into new inquiry and realistic thought about their country and its place in the world. These men, known as the "Generation of '98," were to make a great contribution to the establishment of liberal thought and democratic attitudes and the injection of new vitality into Spanish life. One day their work would bring about the downfall of the monarchy and the establishment of the Spanish republic—and that in itself would bring consequences which are still not completely resolved.

As for the men involved . . .

Admiral Montojo, who had been forced into taking command in a hopeless situation, was arrested upon his return to Spain. The old veteran made a dignified defense (to which Admiral Dewey contributed) against charges brought forward at his court-martial. But this too was a losing battle. Montojo had been selected as a scapegoat, and could not escape his fate. He was ultimately sentenced to expulsion from the navy and the loss of all his pensions and rights. That there were those among his comrades who would still do the old man honor for his heroic fight against overwhelming odds was indicated, however, by a letter written to him by Admiral Manuel de la Camara (whose fleet could not reach the Philippines in time to help Montojo): "Dear Patricio," Camara wrote, "The sentence . . . has caused me deep pain . . . may the New Year bring you and yours very different and better days than the last two." The New Year was 1900, and it was also a new century. The new century would not be very old before Don Patricio Montojo y Pasarón, former vice admiral of the Spanish Navy, was dead.

For Admiral Dewey, the years ahead were to be full of honors conferred by a grateful nation. There was the triumphal return aboard the *Olympia* during the late summer of 1899, by way of the Suez Canal and the Mediterranean—Dewey and his ship were extravagantly feted at every port along their route. Then the gala reception at New York City on October 28th and 29th, with the *Olympia* steaming to anchorage in the Hudson River while hundreds of thousands of Americans cheered themselves hoarse. There was the triumphal arch erected on Fifth Avenue; a $10,000 loving cup made by Tiffany's and presented to Dewey by the City of New York; speeches of welcome. There was the special presentation of a sword by Congress and, finally, the creation of the title Admiral of the Navy which was bestowed on Admiral Dewey and which was to be granted to no other American naval officer. Later, there was even to be a short-lived Dewey for President movement.

But if the years brought honors to Dewey (and a new and happy marriage), they also brought work—the vital work of building a new and powerful American navy. The proudly erect figure of the old admiral reporting to his office at the Navy Department every morning became a familiar

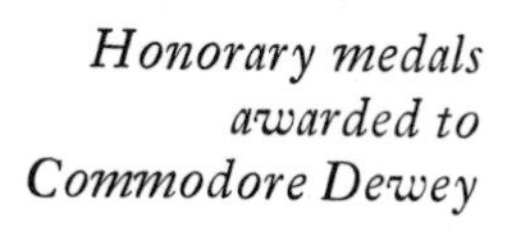
Honorary medals awarded to Commodore Dewey

sight in Washington. How thoroughly and well he did his work in the years of the new century was to be demonstrated when the United States was able to speedily mobilize a vast, efficient fleet for the First World War. But although Dewey had long predicted this conflict, it was one in which he would never engage. On January 11, 1917, the Admiral of the Navy collapsed at his home. When ordered to remain in bed, he protested, half-deliriously: "I'm shirking my duty . . . This nation is faced with a perilous period . . . I must finish my work for my country." But by January 16th, he was deep in a twilight coma. His last words, whispered perhaps to the memory of the grimy men and officers of the ships at Manila Bay, were: "Gentlemen, the battle is done . . . the victory . . . is ours!"

FOR FURTHER READING

DEWEY, ADMIRAL GEORGE. *Autobiography of George Dewey, Admiral of the Navy*. New York: 1913.

FISKE, ADMIRAL BRADLEY A. *War Time in Manila*. Boston: 1913.

FREIDEL, FRANK. *The Splendid Little War*. Boston: 1958.

HEALY, LAURIN HALL & LUIS KUTNER. *The Admiral*. Chicago & New York: 1944.

LONG, JOHN DAVIS. *The New American Navy* (2 vols.). New York: 1903.

MILLIS, WALTER. *The Martial Spirit*. Boston: 1931.

ROOSEVELT, THEODORE. *An Autobiography*. New York: 1913.

SARGENT, NATHAN. *Admiral Dewey and the Manila Campaign*. Washington: 1947.

VIVIAN, THOMAS JONDRIE. *With Dewey at Manila*. New York: 1898.

WEST, RICHARD SEDGEWICK, JR. *Admirals of American Empire*. Indianapolis: 1948.

WILSON, HERBERT WRIGLEY. *The Downfall of Spain*. Boston: 1900.

INDEX

Aguinaldo, Emilio, 67–69, 73–74, 81; *see also* Filipino rebels
Alfonso XIII, King of Spain, 18
American Expeditionary Force, 69; seizes Guam, 72; in Philippines, 72, 74, 76
Asiatic squadron, U.S. Navy, 1–3, 12, 14, 23, 27, 29, 38, 41, 43–45, 47–49, 53–58, 61–64, 74–76

Bacoor Bay, 39, 42
Baker Island, U.S. seizes, 82
Baltimore, USS, 1, 3, 6, 14, 23, 39, 41, 45–46, 48–49, 53–57
battleships, steel, 32–39; conditions aboard, 35, 46–47; means of command, 36–38
Beranger, Admiral, 18, 21–22
Boston, USS, 1, 7, 41, 46

Cadarso, Luis, 28, 52
Camara, Manuel de la, 61–62, 84
Castilla (Sp. ship), 22, 27, 42, 49, 52–53
Cavite Naval Arsenal, 27, 39–42, 48, 52–53, 57–58, 61, 69
Cervera, Pascual, 61
Charleston, USS, 62, 72, 74
Civil War, U.S., 3, 8, 33
Concha, Juan de la, 29, 53
Concord, USS, 1, 7, 41
Corregidor Island, 2–4, 7, 16–17, 23, 28, 35, 61, 64, 79

Cuba, 11, 13–14, 21, 29, 38, 61, 67

Davila, Basilio Augustin, 25, 28, 57, 59–60, 73
Dewey, George: Admiral of the Navy, 84; in Battle of Manila Bay, 40–41, 43–46, 53–56, 58, 61, 79–81, 83; in Battle of Manila City, 59–67, 73–76, 81; career pre-Manila Bay, 8, 33; childhood, 7–8; commands Asiatic squadron, 1–3, 6–7, 12, 14–16, 23, 27, 38; education, 8, 18; and Filipino rebels, 67–69, 74; honors post-Manila Bay, 61, 84–85
Don Antonio de Ulloa (Sp. ship), 42, 57–58
Don Juan de Austria (Sp. ship), 27, 29, 42
Dyer, Nehemiah, 3, 6, 39, 45, 53

El Fraile Island, 4, 6–7, 16–17, 23
Ellicott, John, 3–4, 6, 39, 45, 48–49, 53

Far Eastern fleet, Spanish Navy, 2–3, 7, 13, 17–18, 38–39, 42, 47–49, 57–58, 61
Farragut, David, 3, 7–8, 79
Filipino rebels, 18, 21, 38, 66–67, 73–74, 81
Fiske, Bradley, 6, 35, 40, 45
Fort San Augustin, 75

Generation of '98, 83

Germany in Far East, 64, 81
Gridley, Charles, 6, 41, 45
Guam, U.S. seizes, 72, 82

Hawaii, U.S. annexes, 82
Hay, John, 8
Hearst, William Randolph, 11
Hong Kong, 14, 16, 23, 67–69
Howland Island, U.S. seizes, 82

imperialism: Japanese, 81; U.S., 11, 21, 28–29
Isla de Cuba (Sp. ship), 22, 27, 42–43, 49, 52, 56–57
Isla de Luzon (Sp. ship), 22, 27, 42, 49, 53

Jaudenes, Fermin, 73–74, 76

Lodge, Henry Cabot, 11
Luzon Island, 1, 64

MacArthur, Arthur, 72
Maine, USS, 13–14, 21, 46
Manila, 4, 7, 23, 28, 39–41, 58–61, 69; "battle" for city, 74–76, 81; Spanish surrender, 76
Manila Bay, 2, 16–17, 26–27, 39, 53, 58, 61, 64, 67, 72; defenses, 3–4, 7, 15–23, 27, 39; Dewey's plan for entering, 3–4; *see also* Corregidor, El Fraile
Manila Bay, Battle of: consequences, 61, 81–85; effect on U.S.-Asian relations, 81–83; Spanish casualties, 49–53, 58; steel battleships, 32; U.S. casualties, 35, 56, 58
Maria Cristina, Regent of Spain, 18
Marques del Duero (Sp. ship), 27, 42, 49, 53, 57
McCulloch, Hugh, USS, 1, 4, 6–7, 35, 42
McKinley, William, 11, 61, 69
Merrimac, CSS, 33
Merritt, Wesley, 69, 74
Midway Island, U.S. seizes, 82
Miles, Nelson, 69
Monadnock, USS, 62, 74
Monitor, USS, 33
Monocacy, USS, 14
Monterey, USS, 62, 74
Montojo y Pasarón, Patricio, 18; in Battle of Manila Bay, 42, 52, 56–58; commands Far Eastern fleet, 17, 22–25, 27–28, 39; court-martial, 83–84; lack of war matériel, 22–26, 38; surrenders Manila, 76

Nanshan, USS, 1, 14, 42, 69
Navy, British, 14, 16, 66–67, 75, 81–82
Navy, German, 62–67, 75, 81–82
Navy, Spanish, 1, 17–18, 38–39, 61
Navy, U.S. 1, 8, 33–38, 62, 81–85; mercenaries in, 21–22
Nelson, Horatio, 38

Olympia, USS, 1–4, 6, 14, 23, 34, 40–41, 45–47, 53–56, 58, 60, 74, 76, 84
Oregon, USS, 23

Petrel, USS, 1, 6, 36, 40–41, 45, 58
Philippines, 1, 11, 14, 21, 59, 64, 69, 76, 81–83; Spanish defense, 12–13, 22; *see also* Manila Bay, Filipino rebels
Primo de Rivera, Miguel, 25–26, 67

Raleigh, USS, 1, 7, 41, 46
Redondo, Dr. Juan, 42–43, 52, 56
Reina Cristina (Sp. ship), 22, 27–29, 42, 49, 52–53
Roosevelt, Theodore, 9–10, 14, 69

Sangley Point, 57
Sino-Japanese War, 32
Sostoa, Enrique, 57
Spanish-American War, 13–14, 21, 67; armistice, 76; causes, 11
Spanish government, 18–21, 76, 83; *see also* Filipino rebels
Stickney, Joseph, 2, 4, 45–46
Subic Bay, 1–2, 17, 28; defenses, 25, 27

U.S. government, 9–11, 14, 33–34, 67–69, 76, 81–83, 85; *see also* American Expeditionary Force; Asiatic squadron; imperialism; Navy, U.S.; Spanish-American War

Von Diedrichs, Admiral, 64–67, 75, 81

Wake Island, U.S. seizes, 82
Wilhelm II, Kaiser of Germany, 64
World War I, 64, 85

Zafiro, USS, 1, 14, 42, 60